Jonathan Ketchum
Oakstone Farm
9905 Brauer Road
Clarence Center, N. Y. 14032

25578

120

091

Philosophical Explorations
Edited by George Kimball Plochmann

Plato's *Meno*

A Philosophy of Man as Acquisitive

Robert Sternfeld and Harold Zyskind

Foreword by George Kimball Plochmann

Southern Illinois University Press
Carbondale and Edwardsville

Carbondale and Edwardsville
Feffer & Simons, Inc. / London and Amsterdam

Dedicated to Richard McKeon

who has proved to us that in philosophy knowledge is power and that both are intrinsically bound up with the vitality of past thought, the enrichment of present methodical thought, and the prospective insights into the possibilities of ever evolving thought.

Library of Congress Cataloging in Publication Data

Sternfeld, Robert.
  Plato's Meno: a philosophy of man as acquisitive.

  (Philosophical explorations)
  Includes bibliographical references and index.
  1. Plato. Meno.   I. Zyskind, Harold, joint author.
II. Series.
B377.S73   170   77–25446
ISBN 0–8093–0838–X

Printed in the United States

Designed by David Ford

Contents

Foreword

The world of the *Meno* is a relatively small one, and its concerns pertain to a narrow band in Athenian and Thessalian society. There is, for example, scarcely a hint of interest in the social status of the slave-boy; he merely exhibits a transition from ignorance to right opinion. Unlike the world of the *Republic* or even the *Laws*, this world is evidently one in which hearsay instruction, prejudice, and lack of sound family tradition all cut a large figure. But if this world is narrow it is not unduly so, for it has connections with the everyday life of other times and places. Professors Sternfeld and Zyskind make, stress, and then illustrate the point that while Plato is writing about men of Athens and Larisa, he is at the same time using these city-states to exemplify broader movements in human experience, movements repeatable times without number. If you say that the recurrences will not be identical then this objection helps to explain why Plato refrains from offering more than a bare sketch of personages and conditions he thinks typical of the lives he is depicting. Details of the food to be eaten and the music to be danced to can be laid out for the best or second-best state; but where one is describing weaknesses of actual society and hinting that these are likely to turn up anywhere, it is prudent to be sparing of concrete description, for with it one will lose all hope of attaining this degree of generality.

The chief contention of this book is that in the *Meno* Plato looks for problems restricted in scope yet still open in their implications, and seeks a method for making them intelligible, or at any rate more manageable. He does this by connecting them with what is already known or with conceptual structures suitable for the occasions at hand. It is a method of playing by ear. To find a link between disparate things—Plato believes that this can be done in the sphere of action ethically, educationally, and politically conceived; but the price to be paid is that we must remodel science, *epistēmē*, in terms of direct acquaintance, contact, *gignoskein;* and we must be satisfied with something that the *Republic* would disdain, namely opinion. If we can establish a modicum of harmony in a time of troubles, which is all times, then this is much to the good, even if we must for present purposes dispense with axioms, demonstrations, and with a correspondent realm of pure, unalterable essences. In the local applications which Plato makes, the method seeks intermediaries and compromises; nevertheless the attentive reader can no doubt discern in the dialogue an aid to reflection and to right action when his own many-sided predicaments obtrude.

Euthyphro: . . . Somehow everything that we put forward keeps moving about, and nothing will stay where we set it.
Socrates: The things you have said, Euthyphro, look like the work of Daedalus, my progenitor.

Euthyphro 11b–c

The *Meno* has often been criticized for being ambiguous, or if not that, inconclusive, offering a lame and needless concession to popular morals, much like the controversial passage in the *Protagoras,* in which Socrates evidently upholds an ethic based upon calculation of pleasures and pains. To defend the *Meno* from these charges by citing the arguments whereby the present book speaks on its behalf would be to anticipate uselessly, but any less thorough recital would unfortunately beg two questions at once: Plato is right if the commentary can show he is right, and Sternfeld and Zyskind are right if their book fits the lessons of the *Meno*. One can, however, say this much: If Plato thinks that in the somewhat disjointed world of the Athenians and Thessalians the most feasible political ethic builds by using what we already have, and shows the special resources of right opinion in conjunction with a compatible conception of knowledge, then responsible commentators are obviously required to find this in the text. And if Plato is moreover thinking about human life in general, not merely a couple of Greek provinces, then the commentators do well to glance at what is, or passes for, right opinion in our day—operationism, utilitarianism, pragmatism, relativism, to name four prevailing views. This very act of connecting Athens with modern Europe and America might seem a blurring of issues, a letting of the words of Plato's text run off in all directions. A philosophical principle, however, is not spoiled by applying it as widely as its component concepts and its structure will permit, and certainly one clarifies its real sense upon learning to use it oneself.

Eleatic Stranger: . . . If an argument, even though lengthy, makes the hearer more able to find the truth, we should eagerly accept it and not take offense; or, if it be shorter, we should do the same.

Statesman 286e

Messrs. Sternfeld and Zyskind have not composed a line-by-line commentary, such as one finds in several current books on the *Meno*, nor have they adopted the still more popular extreme of writing on "themes" in that work. Instead they have sought just the combination of the two which they deemed would best enable their readers to see the philosophical connections between statements often cropping up at wide remove from each other in the dialogue. Again, there are connections, not identities in the text; and the result is that our interpreters have tried to uncover the fuller, richer, and at the same time more precise significations which Plato has been able to instill in his own words. Sternfeld and Zyskind have wisely employed multiple approaches to the same topic or term, to insure that no one connection dominates throughout and gives the term a false show of "technical" fixity of meaning. They treat of psychological aspects of what is said by the participants, of the purely formal aspects, the historical, the ethical, political, mathematical, and, yes, the metaphysical, though they are equally careful not to keep *these* as fixed distinctions any more than they have deemed the original statements to have unique interpretations that can be settled once and for all. They assume that the *Meno* makes sense in many ways, or on many levels, if you prefer, but also that it has a unity underlying all these aspects. The authors are like a man who runs several knives through a melon, each blade piercing and in a sense connecting two parts of the same rind, regardless of the individual direction it may take. Messrs. Sternfeld and Zyskind do not fall into the trap of construing any passage in the dialogue and then storing it away in the belief that this passage need not be returned to several times and reconsidered in light of subsequent formulations of the same—or even seemingly distantly related—points. Or, to vary the image, the two authors are like an operator of several colored searchlights beamed upon a neutral wall, searchlights whose rays are added to each other to produce a searing focal center for a number of them together. The multiple readings of the *Meno* sum into a coherent whole, but it is not a monochrome whole.

Crito: Who was it, Socrates, with whom you were talking yesterday in the Lyceum?. . . . Who was he?
Socrates: . . . There were two of them, not one.

Euthydemus 271a

   In coming to the main body of this thoughtful study, one feels that it must have been the work of a single mind. Only after glancing at the prefatory statement of joint authorship would it be evident that there were two writers, so seamlessly have they woven the fabric of their account of the *Meno*. Most scholars prefer to go their separate ways, or else, try as they may, they are unable to enter into harmonious thinking. At most they will engage in what are euphemistically called symposia, or erroneously called dialogues simply because the travel expenses are paid from a common pocket. Here instead we have two men, one of whom has previously published chiefly upon the philosophy of rhetoric, the other upon the philosophy of mathematics, combining their efforts in the searching, intense, and fruitful discussions of which we see only the end-product here. So far as I can see, they are at home in a world that Plato never made nor knew, but whose frailties and vices and enormous strengths would seem closely to resemble his own.

George Kimball Plochmann

Southern Illinois University at Carbondale
16 March 1977

Preface

In our study of Plato's *Meno* we have found a philosophic structure which has provided us with a perspective on much twentieth-century philosophy. This structure and perspective are results of philosophizing by interpretation. Such a practice raises two general questions: First, what are the grounds for defending our interpretation against others, besides the indispensable claim of adding to present understanding? Second, can one do philosophy properly by interpreting another writer's text?

As for the second, though proper philosophizing is often thought to be concerned with problems currently pursued and with solutions reached through modes accepted these days, present problems and modes of thought may be grasped in a new way by means of insight attained in the interpretation of older texts. This second question will be explored in chapter 9 where the perspective derived from the *Meno* is used for viewing aspects of contemporary philosophy. We devote this preface rather to the first question, to provide preliminary general grounds for our interpretation in comparison with others.

Among the least satisfactory interpretations of Plato's dialogues are those which cannot explicate certain portions of a dialogue and reject whole passages as uninterpretable because our thoughts today diverge too much from those of fourth-century Greece. Others apply conventional conceptions of Platonism in order to prove Plato's real rejection of what he is evidently presenting in the text at hand. Still others use contemporary standards of philosophizing to bind Plato's arguments to inapplicable criteria. Once we have eliminated these obviously unsatisfactory efforts there is no conclusive way to prove that a single account of a Platonic dialogue is a final or best interpretation. Even if one does adopt Coleridge's principle that when "baffled in all attempts to understand the ignorance of Plato, I CONCLUDE MYSELF IGNORANT OF HIS UNDERSTANDING,"[1] there is still the problem of determining which application of this principle yields a more adequate account of a Platonic dialogue. Typically, Gilbert Ryle has criticized other interpreters for their not having taken Plato's own words seriously enough,[2] while his interpretation has been criticized in turn, as being wide of the mark.

There is no way to establish a definitive relationship between the words read and some privileged semantical grounds for them; hence the coexistence of diverse philosophical interpretations is regarded as normal. The claim can also be made in science that different paradigms are incommensurable. Nevertheless, though differences in philosophical textual interpretation are not finally decidable they are usefully arguable. They have enough textual facts and theoretic issues in common to make critical give-and-take both intelligible and effective, even though often it only reflects and extends the original differences.

On these assumptions we will here press the claims of the kind of interpretation we have made. In the first place most interpreters of the *Meno* could agree in some ambiguous sense that the dialogue employs a diversity of methods and that it does not explicitly show a steady movement toward a synthesizing overview. This has been treated variously, often illuminatingly if not with enough boldness. It also has led some to deny that the dialogue has philosophic content at all,[3] or else to assert that it is a cruder presentation of "the characteristic metaphysics of the *Phaedo*."[4] We regard this diversity of methods and the dialogue's "descending" dialectic (i.e., the movement from definition and recollection downward to opinion) as in themselves its essential characteristics, explaining the construction of the dialogue as Plato's effort to show the minimal elements of philosophic content in thought and action. When we view it as the presentation of an irreducible minimum, we see it as compatible with other Platonic doctrines without being a weak imitation of them; and the irreducibility of the diverse methods means that their relations to each other are not primarily competitive or hierarchical but pluralistic. Our effort to deal straightforwardly with the dialogue's diversity rather than seek either a reconciling concept or an ironic explanation of it admittedly creates some problems, but we believe we can show the latter to be more manageable than those generated in other treatments.

Although this interpretation does not follow uniquely from the internal analysis we have employed, it is certainly occasioned by it. This has not prevented us of course from appreciating and using insights achieved by interpretations made mainly in other modes (e.g., Jacob Klein's distinguished linear and linguistic commentary), but the main point is that just as our structural approach by no means predetermines a particular interpretation so also it does not and is not intended to free us from confronting issues highlighted by alternative approaches. This mutual confrontation is necessary to the philosophic give-and-take we noted earlier. For a broader defense then, we add some notes here on our treatment of certain alternatives.

A major alternative is of course historical analysis. Gilbert Ryle, for instance, makes much of the historical probability, external to the dialogues themselves, that Plato was himself a participant in eristic tournaments. This leads Ryle into misleading simplifications of both the argument and the drama of the dialogue, but more than this is his neglect of another external fact—Socrates' great love of Athens and his gratitude for her having provided him with the conditions of the philosophic life. This second fact is needed to explain why in the *Meno* Socrates is so tolerant of some Athenian leaders whom he censures in other contexts. As gadfly and torpedo fish Socrates harassed Athens, but it was the freedom of Athens that made this way of life possible. That fact also supplies the external justification for his "reliance" on Anytos in the *Meno*. We clearly depend on these external facts even though we do not biographically detail them. The interesting issue on this point is not structure versus history but which historical facts are significant?

Again, while approaches vary in which features they identify as drama/poetry and which as argument/logic, and in whether a separate analysis may be made of each, the issues here often tend to be abstract problems of definition. The theoretically significant differences on this between say, Robert S. Brumbaugh and John Herman Randall, Jr., do not directly cause their differences in interpretation and do not reduce the excellence of either. In practice we, like many others, often directly follow the dialogue's tendency to associate propositions with speakers' characters. We also nonetheless treat drama and argument as analytically separable, seeking the unity of the plot and the logic of the argument. Our emphasis falls on the latter; but, as indicated, these questions of emphasis and formal separability are only at the edges of the interesting interpretive issues. Some scholars who vary on these yet agree that in the *Meno* dramatic features significantly alter, or even reverse, the surface meaning of propositional arguments. For us, on the other hand, drama and argument reciprocally reinforce each other. We believe this to be a discovered relation, reasonable but not imposed. This reinforcement further is not a matter of echoed meanings but of complementary filling out. For example, when we find that the discursive argument shows that virtue is not teachable because of the fluidity and magnitude of the context in which men take future-directed action, we also find that the plot gives this magnitude additional meaning by showing dramatically that the concept of virtue resists efforts of poets or sophists to catch it as a "matter" within their supposedly universal forms. In sum, while our main interest has restricted the poetic analysis in our study, it has stimulated us to try to pin down the way these elements interact with the logic of the dialogue to yield a unified meaning.

We do not interpret the dialogues' meanings as relative to their temporal order. But we discriminate the problems appearing in different dialogues, each of which purports to treat the same or overlapping subjects; for example, *Laches, Phaedrus, Protagoras*. We give each dialogue its own lead, as it were, and the complementary relations we thus establish build up a nexus which we present as defensible on its own. We thus readily entertain the ancient tradition, revived by G. K. Plochmann, that Plato reworked his dialogues concurrently, while we use the labels "earlier" and "later" dialogues in the modern fashion.[5]

We have been wary of relying too much on conventional Platonic or other accepted meanings of terms. We have sought mainly to tie meaning to use by comparison and contrast with other Platonic uses. We draw, for example, some inferences from the contrast discussed in chapter 8 between the truncated use of "dialectic" in the *Meno* and its more fully elaborate structure in other dialogues; we also explore disparate meanings of "virtue" within the dialogue as well as by contrast with uses in other dialogues. There is no doubt that subtle linguistic and hermeneutic analyses can reveal features not caught in our analysis; but in the respects indicated our method may do more justice to the words of Plato.

It comes to this: We do not interpret the *Meno* as no more than a particular instance of some conception of Plato's broad philosophic position. However, on the question of understanding a dialogue by the bearing on it of arguments found in other dialogues, we argue the compatibility of the *Meno* with the content of other dialogues even as we insist on the unique contribution of the *Meno*. No one knowing the Platonic letters and all the dialogues except the *Meno* could predict the content and method of that work. Yet knowing them all, one could say retrospectively that the *Meno* fills a conspicuous gap.

Thus our interpretation speaks to the same questions raised by other techniques of inquiry into the text. We believe it studies the internal structure of the dialogue intensively enough to give new significance to the issue of the dialogue's own contribution to action and thought. We argue that Plato's focus in the *Meno* makes this dialogue more immediately relevant than are the others to Athens' practical situation, and that its ultimate concern is with the concrete future of the state and philosophy rather than with an intellectual problem as such. But this concern is applicable to any state and the state of philosophy at any given time. So, without undue expansion of the *Meno*'s significance, we believe it suggests three critical needs of our own time: the need to recognize how much the future depends on a continuing supply of able men to exercise world leadership, rather than the triumph of some special view of scientific method or of one ideal society; the indispensability of hope as a motive force in the search for them; and finally, the need for a major turn in philosophy which can take us beyond this minimal philosophy without distorting the basic values on which the *Meno* shows man's world to rest— however precariously—even today.

This book began as a short critical article on current interpretations of the slave-boy episode—particularly the interpretations of Malcolm Brown and Gregory Vlastos. It has evolved through numerous revisions in response to criticisms and suggestions of friends who most graciously contributed their time and effort. In this process, most of our critical comments about other interpretations have been drastically cut in order to conform to space restrictions and to present more cogently our own developing insights.

Walter Watson read an early version of the book and contributed helpful suggestions, including the point that we should omit lengthy analyses of others' interpretations. Glenn R. Morrow graciously responded to a request from Sternfeld for criticism. He made numerous suggestions for improvement including helpful details on our citation of Greek words and phrases and more general admonitions for a more imaginative and persuasive presentation. George Kimball Plochmann reviewed our work on a purely friendly basis before he undertook the additional task of being its official editor in his series, Philosophical Explorations. Our arguments and expressions benefited by his unusual combination of philosophic and literary talents—a combination which has made his series one in which we are honored to have our book included. Robert S. Brumbaugh read the whole typescript somewhere in midstream and contributed materially. The criticisms of these men had an effect not only on details of expression, but upon the final shape in which the argument is presented.

In addition, we had discussions with Leonard Olsen, David Benfield, and Nathaniel Lawrence on various points in the dialogue. Further, we corresponded with Brumbaugh on the dramatic aspect of the dialogue, with Hippocrates G. Apostle on some points in the geometrical illustration of the argument-by-hypothesis, and with Abram V. Martin on the history of early Greek mathematics. We are indebted to all these persons for stimulating interchanges, though we are responsible for the readings we express here.

Eddy Zemach read an earlier version of our chapter on General Paragenics and saved us from serious error in our account of some twentieth-century philosophies. By no means least are those friends who provided many useful suggestions which substantially improved our expression and argument: Bruce Bashford, David H. Chandler, Homer Goldberg, Ann Hoffman, and especially Thomas Rogers.

Our greatest debt is to Richard McKeon, not only for providing us with the rich philosophic background out of which this study developed, but for an extended meeting on the typescript which became the occasion for placing the *Meno* as both an instance and a distinctive use of Platonic dialectic.

We are especially indebted to all those who not only gave valuable criticism, but encouraged us to develop further, this interpretation. This support has indeed been heartening and helpful.

Sternfeld acknowledges gratefully the Summer Faculty Fellowships (1971, 1973) provided by the Research Foundation of the State University of New York for work on this book. Zyskind owes special thanks to Henry Rosenberg and Larry Roberts for generous and able technical assistance in the preparation of copy.

It gives us much pleasure finally to express our gratitude to Mrs. Joseph G. Quinn for her expert typing through many revisions and for her good cheer and interest as well as efficiency throughout.

Each of us is primary author of the chapters indicated: Zyskind, chapters 1, 5, 6, and 8; Sternfeld, chapters 2, 4, 7, and 9. We contributed about equally to chapter 3. This statement is a general guide, as both of us have taken a hand in almost every chapter. For example, Zyskind wrote a sizable part of chapter 9, and Sternfeld part of chapter 8.

Robert Sternfeld
Harold Zyskind

Stony Brook, N.Y.
April 25, 1977

Part One: The Boundary Conditions of the Problem

1 Introduction: The Dialogue as Drama

Platonic idealism as traditionally understood[1] sets up a hierarchy of values and cognitions determined by eternal ideas existing independently of man's mind or physical nature. Most dialogues dominated by Socrates are reasonably if incompletely interpreted as explorations of some aspect of this idealism. In obvious ways the *Meno* fits the pattern, beginning as it does with a search for a definition of virtue which Meno's conventional opinions cannot supply (71B–80B— referred to here as pt. I), and then establishing the familiar doctrine of recollection to provide a warrant for renewing the search for a definition (80C–86C—referred to here as pt. II). But after that the *Meno* shifts radically. The search for the definition is abandoned with little ado; instead an inquiry is made into the way virtue is acquired (86E–100B—referred to here as pt. III). For Socrates this is a logically posterior problem—asking and answering a *poion*-form question, what a quality of a thing is, before dealing with the prior *ti*-form question, what a thing is. (Note his remarks at 71B, 86B, 100B.)

From the standpoint of the divided line of *Republic* VI, an initial *poion* inquiry could well open the way to the essential definitional

3

question. The *Meno* reverses this order, however, and in the final section (86E–100B), the participants do proceed *successfully* without either knowing or actively seeking a definition. In the process Socrates develops a theory of action and politics dependent on public opinion and justified by its consequences rather than by its conceptual grounds. In this sense the emphasis, in current vocabulary, becomes "operationist"—testing by the effects—and the same emphasis is evident in other logical and epistemological devices employed in the inquiry. For example, one of Socrates' first moves in the *poion* inquiry is to deny the distinction he had insisted on earlier between being taught and recollecting (87C). When the earlier "idealist" sections are viewed retrospectively, after we have read through the dialogue, certain operationist and empirical features in these sections take on added importance; for example, that Socrates talks about geometrical problems with a slave-boy who lacks a developed capacity for abstract thought.

As many scholars have tried to show, interpretive skill and a moderate respect for the Platonic corpus can "explain" these operationist features and thereby bring the *Meno* into line by dating the dialogue early enough, or by accentuating Socrates' irony, or by discovering implicit idealist meanings. Such explanations, however, generate as many difficulties as they resolve, for they depend upon strongly discounting the face value of the arguments.

We take the contrary view that in the *Meno* Plato is breaking new ground, developing what may be called an idealist operationism which has its own rationale. What this expression means, and whether it is really applicable can be decided only by a detailed analysis. We can suggest its practical import here, however, by a comparison with the *Apology*, a dialogue also concerned, though in a different way, with the prosecution of Socrates (Anytos cuts a figure in both works). In the *Apology* Socrates calls on the Athenians to reverse their order of values, and he ridicules Athens' politicians. No such change is sought or envisaged in the *Meno*, and the problem is seen rather as one of insuring the continuity of the sort of virtue which leading Athenian politicians have possessed and which has stood as the basis of the freedom Athens has maintained for decades.

(i)   *Some Current Criticisms of the* Meno

In the context of Plato's philosophy as a whole the approach of the *Meno* must be confined to a limited role, and within the dialogue Socrates emphasizes the limitations of some of the arguments, especially in the culminating section which gives priority to the *poion* question; clarity, he says, will *not* be attained until the *ti* question is answered (100B). But within these limitations the key arguments of the dialogue stand unrefuted. No internal weakness in the *poion* section (pt. III) is indicated. In general, Socrates' attitude toward the argument shows the same (two) complementary sides found in many dialogues—Socrates' own reserve about the extent or finality of the argument accompanies his reliance on it in good faith once its boundaries are recognized. Even in the role of the absolutist in the *Phaedo*, Socrates warns against the twin dangers of certitude and misology. The difficulty in understanding the *Meno* arises not from inherent ambiguities in the status of its argument but from our own reluctance to accredit a Platonic operationism and to attend to it as sympathetically as Socrates himself does in the dialogue.

The difficulty is evident in the previously mentioned tendency among commentators to explain away possible positive significance in the *poion* section of the dialogue. R. G. Hoerber finds it "illogical" on many counts;[2] he explains such aberrations by saying that Plato's dramatic purpose is to expose Meno and Anytos.[3] Similarly Jacob Klein sees the pre-*poion* sections of the dialogue as unmasking Meno's depravity and ignorance (*amathia*) and then describes Socrates' own effort (98B ff.) to summarize the *poion* section as bringing "no more light . . . to bear on the subject."[4] Victor Goldschmidt finds the dialogue at 89C not serious.[5] Other commentators do not explain away arguments but discount them nonetheless by claiming that what Socrates is doing here does not commit him to positions different from those he takes elsewhere. Thus F. Schleiermacher sees irony[6] and Klein sees sarcasm[7] in Socrates' praise of leaders whom he censures in other dialogues. A passage in the *poion* section which has attracted most attention is the adaptation of a hypothetical method taken from geometry to the question of how virtue is acquired (86E–89E). Generally, however, commentators on this passage have interpreted and criticized its method on the standard of the quite different hypothetical reasoning developed in the *Phaedo* and the *Republic*; H.-P. Stahl even sees it as "essentially" an effort, though not yet successful, to grasp firmly "the essence of virtue"—the *ti* question.[8]

The pre-*poion* sections on definition and recollection fare better in the commentaries, except where they exhibit prominent operationist features, and then commentators have used various means to render these sections compatible with favored Platonic doctrines. Gilbert Ryle treats them as illustrating skill in logical tournaments; for him, Plato's development of substantive philosophic positions is left to later dialogues.[9] Both Bernard Phillips[10] and Gregory Vlastos[11] make the slave-boy episode into a reassertion of the Platonic distinction between the intellectual and the sensible. They do this in different ways, but both ignore the fact that Socrates nowhere in the argument makes anything of this idealist distinction. Malcolm Brown[12] argues that this episode, as well as the final section, is intended to show us examples of bad reasoning.

Despite such efforts to explain them away, the operationist features of the sections on definition and recollection remain critical, accounting in good measure for the fact that these sections of the *Meno* attract much interest in contemporary discussions. Richard M. Hare finds the doctrine of recollection as exhibited in the slave-boy episode useful in understanding how philosophical discovery escapes the bare analytic-synthetic distinction.[13] Alexander Sesonske finds the *Meno* useful in developing linguistically oriented relations of saying and knowing.[14] The treatment of definitions in the *Meno* similarly lends itself well to the modern frame employed by Richard Robinson in *Plato's Earlier Dialectic*,[15] and is at least suggestive for Laura Grimm's " 'reconstruction' . . . from the point of view of a modern logician" in her *Definition in Plato's Meno*.[16] The range of interests sparked by the operationist focus is suggested further by the titles of Ernan McMullin's "Insight and the *Meno*"[17] and of Ira Cohen's "Programmed Learning and the Socratic Dialogue."[18]

Thus the first two parts of the dialogue are drawing the major attention both of Platonic scholars and of those who find the dialogue relevant to contemporary problems. But as we have indicated, in our view the *Meno* is a homogeneous argument, culminating in the *poion* section, which deals with problems of both logic and action that abandon reliance on definitions or essences in favor of hypothetical, heuristic, and empirical considerations. Only by breaking away from the assumption that Plato would not make such an analysis primary, and by taking seriously the methods and doctrines which are left unrefuted, can we see the distinctive features of the *Meno*.

This analysis is, for Plato, a distinctive philosophic approach, a new way of generating and treating problems. It centers on the question of the ways in which diverse and discrete entities become joined in self-enclosed unions within any area, whether the topic be mathematics (recollection part) or politics and the formation of public opinion (*poion* part). Further, the analysis seeks the relation of objects not in overarching concepts or in an ontological hierarchy but simply in links or "fits" determined in different ways by the objects themselves as man thinks about, experiences, or projectively conjoins them. The question put by Meno which opens the dialogue sets up man and virtue as two nominally discrete entities to be connected (How does virtue accrue to or come beside man? [*paragignetai*—70A]). In the succeeding arguments the modes of connection between man and diverse objects of awareness, and between the objects themselves, are elaborated as a basis for dealing with Meno's opening question. We call the philosophic approach which the dialogue develops *paragenics*,[19] following Plato's verbal lead. Being broadly concerned with the problem of how to bring entities into relation, paragenics for Plato obviously has its roots in idealism; yet it is particularly open in seeking to relate entities which may not be subject to systematic treatment. These have thus to be joined operationally, that is, by means which succeed rather than conform to a set intellectual standard. Because the search is one of this kind it aims at piecemeal solutions rather than at the dialectically comprehensive schemes commonly associated with Plato.

We intend these summary statements about the dialogue and paragenics to be no more than suggestive; they must be specified, elaborated, and defended, and that is the task of this book. Chapters 2 through 7 reconstruct the principles and methods of the *Meno* through analysis of the three major parts of the dialogue: the definition section (pt. I of the dialogue), the slave-boy episode (pt. II), and the *poion* section (pt. III). Chapter 8 traces the continuity of linguistic and structural strands that run through the work as a whole. But first, we must take note of one of the pervasive characteristics of all Platonic dialogues as found in the *Meno*—its dramatic structure. We do this in anticipation of the total argument for three reasons: (1) Other commentators have misused this element to explain away their difficulties with the logic. This misuse must be brought into question. (2) The dramatic structure is itself a basic strand in the dialogue as a whole and deserves full development. (3) The dramatic structure must be seen as interwoven with the logic of the total argument and the details which emerge section by section.

(ii)   *The Dramatic Unity of the* Meno—*Its Plot*

Most commentaries on the dramatic aspect of the dialogue deal with selected passages *ad hoc*, generally for the purpose of accounting for anomalies in the argument. However, Jacob Klein's account of the *Meno*'s drama goes far in finding a single action that turns on the person of Meno—the unmasking of his *amathia*.[20] Apart from whether this interpretation is accurate, it has two formal difficulties. First, the unmasking is climactically accomplished by the end of the slave-boy episode, so that part III (the *poion* section) would become a mere epilogue. Second, even if the question were "Who is Meno?" as Klein says it is,[21] this query still does not indicate the core of the drama. While the identity of the protagonist is indeed the *question* in Sophocles' *Oedipus Rex*, the *drama* is in the change wrought in Oedipus by the revelation of his identity. The drama of the *Meno* is, similarly, not in exposing his identity, but in showing what happens to him.

Gilbert Ryle classifies the *Meno* with what he terms the pre-philosophical eristic dialogues, thus making the dramatic action consist in the demolition of an opponent.[22] Meno does make eristic statements to Socrates (75C and 80D), and his opening question, as Klein says, is a challenge to Socrates, but it is misleading to view these questions as step-by-step logical jousting. The paradigm before Meno's mind, as Socrates presents it (70B) and as Meno's several remarks show (76C), is that of Gorgias' boldly answering any question. Meno's opening query in effect invites a comparable display from Socrates and challenges him in that sense. Meno is quick to express his pleasure when Socrates gives a model definition he likes (76E); he does not have to be tamed into a yes-man, as does Thrasymachus, but treats the answers to his eristic questions as opportunities to draw Socrates out (81E). In overemphasizing the role of eristic in the dialogue, Ryle has missed the flow of the argument and the dramatic cues. The dialogue does not open with a challenge and end with a final victory. It opens with Meno's asking his question on how virtue is acquired and ends with his getting an answer. This mere question-answer sequence could not be the main action, but the main action has to take it into account and be compatible with it as the verbal framework.

Robert Brumbaugh[23] sees drama as important throughout the dialogue, but on the ground that it reverses the result of the logic by showing Socrates' teaching Meno through shared inquiry. From this instance, he generalizes the contradictory of "No virtue is taught." As previously indicated we find conversely that the logic and drama reciprocally reinforce each other. This will be indicated at a number of points in the present chapter and will be strengthened in each succeeding chapter. We agree with Brumbaugh that Socrates improves those who associate with him, but this is conveyed not merely dramatically but also logically as Socrates quotes Theognis that young men improve by associating with good men of power. But the fact of Meno's agreeing with Socrates, which Brumbaugh stresses, does not explain the specific changes occurring in him, nor does it detail the strategies and the resistances they are designed to deal with. Nor does it touch what in the dialogue is equally important and perhaps more striking—namely, that, as we shall see, Socrates has to make significant readjustments in his own initial criteria of inquiry to produce any change in so limited a person as Meno. We turn now to our own view.

Framework and Problem of the Plot. Between the beginning and the end of the dialogue Meno is brought from a verbal interest in the stock eristic question of how virtue is acquired to the point where this interest becomes at least momentarily substantive and puts him at the threshold of doing a virtuous action. The test of an action's being virtuous is established in this dialogue as lying in its consequences, and the act with which Meno is charged at the end—to persuade Anytos of their conclusion—would meet just this standard, for Socrates' final word is that this act would be useful for Athens.

Our statement above of the plot, is built on the question-answer sequence which we pointed out earlier. The finding which Meno is to carry to Anytos (virtue comes from the gods) is Socrates' answer to Meno's opening question, but unlike Gorgias, Socrates does not answer the question immediately; rather, he parries it to initiate the exchange which will prepare Meno for a politically useful answer to it.

For Meno to reach this later condition in which he entertains at least a passing interest in virtue and in the possibility of acting virtuously is surprising on several counts. This may explain many scholars' neglect of it even though it is clear enough by the time the dialogue closes. We know from external testimony, principally Xenophon's, that Meno and Anytos are "bad" men. There is internal evidence too—Meno's friendship with Aristippus and the "Great King" in the context of wealth-getting (78C–D). There are thus some grounds for E. S. Thompson's argument that "there is no real inconsistency between Plato's picture and that of Xenophon."[24] When Meno's character is viewed retrospectively any affirmative change Socrates may have produced in him is surprising. And the special nature of his questionable morals complicates the matter further. If he were a Callicles or Thrasymachus who had rationalized injustice and power, we could expect the usual Socratic attack against a self-serving rationalization as a form of his basic disposition. The problem in the dialogue consists rather in the untroubled way Meno's questionable moral practices coexist so easily with the lip-service he pays to virtue, using the skill at this learned from Gorgias. These two aspects of Meno's character occasionally meet, of course, as when Meno says that "procuring gold and silver is virtue" (78D). Meno amends this tribute to the customary, morally indeterminate practice by agreeing, when reminded, that the procuring must be just, an amendment which Thrasymachus would reject. These two facts effectively sum up the situation. Meno on his own, has neglected to say "justly," but when reminded he thinks and says "of course." The "of course" is only lip-service to virtue, and so does not lead us to expect the change. The lip-service is important, however, for we will see from hindsight that Socrates uses it as an entry to the possibility of a moral improvement in Meno.

As with Meno's character, so it is with his fondness for the sophistic discourse of Gorgias.[25] He delights in having his questions answered boldly by Gorgias and then in using the answers to make fine speeches (80E). We see a variant of this in the definitional section when he repeats Gorgias' answers by rote initially, and then borrows a poet's definition in the style of Gorgias. Socrates suggests in the opening that this sophistic activity is merely verbal, separable from practice for the Thessalians as manifest in their wealth-getting and horsemanship. Meno's attachment to Gorgias' method and "wisdom," as thus separable and as lending itself to his mimetic addiction, makes any shift into substantive discourse unexpected. But again we can see in hindsight that after Socrates encounters the blocks to his own preferences of method, he finds the means of adapting it. We have noted already that he makes the outer frame of the dialogue mirror the sophistic question-answer format, while he critically extends it, so that at the end Meno has reason to see the Socratic answer, which he is to pass on to Anytos, as having practical consequences.[26] Meno's awareness of the Socratic method as capable of provoking harmful consequences first appears at the end of the definitional section. Socrates is well-advised, Meno says, not to go abroad (80B). Then Meno sees that in Athens itself Socrates arouses the menacing anger of the politician Anytos (95A); and at the close Meno himself speaks of the effect which Socrates' message would have on Anytos (99E). So if the transmission of a Gorgian answer is part of the verbal display in which the Thessalians engage, the Socratic message is more than that. Presumably the benefit to the Athenians in the envisaged gentling of Anytos by Meno would be to divert him from the repressive course, signalized in the *Meno*, which led him to prosecute Socrates.

That a slave-boy should recollect a form of the Pythagorean theorem is no less surprising and, as it turns out, probable, suggesting in turn some probability in Meno's being disposed to do Socrates' bidding at the end. The limited character of this change in Meno may be seen by measuring it against Socrates' indication (by the slave-boy episode) of what authentic action means for him. The root of such action is substantive inquiry as genuinely energetic (81D); its result is to make one better and braver (86C); and finally for Socrates it produces a total actional commitment—he will defend the value of inquiry in word and deed (85C). The action Meno takes falls considerably short of this three-step paradigm. For him even to have attempted it he would minimally have had to join Socrates in the recollective search for what virtue is. Socrates tries twice to draw him into this search, but Meno resists both times and returns to the posterior question of how virtue is acquired, as Socrates perhaps knew he would. Many commentators and readers accordingly give up on Meno. But not Socrates. With the paradigm clearly in the background and guiding, he first sees a need for, and then discovers, a second-best way with its own distinctive merit and capacity to engage Meno. Thus far we have dealt mainly with the outer framework of this way; we turn now to the internal process by which it moves.

Stages of Change in Meno I—To the Peripety. The stages of the action are determined by Socrates' discovering the adjustments he must make in his initial criteria for discourse before he is ready to answer Meno's opening question, and by Meno's being brought to the point of readiness for that answer. In turning the talk initially from acquisition to definition Socrates thereby does not step wholly outside the concerns of Gorgian discourse; for Meno's response is not that the definitional question is strange or merely formalistic, but that the answer is easy. There is a plausible reason for Meno to downgrade the problem of defining virtue: If the "abundant" and "very good" speeches about virtue which he has given elsewhere (80B) are thought of in conventional poetic or rhetorical terms as being made up of a content expressed in a style, then Socrates' question should indeed be easy to answer. He asks only for content. The hard task in Gorgian eloquence is not to identify a content, but to treat it with style.

Socrates' search for virtue as an underlying entity bearing qualities (see chap. 2), reverses the relative significance which Meno is accustomed to assigning content and style. The exchange should show him that virtue is, itself, to be conceived as having within its content the qualities whose attribution to it would make the speech a fine (and true) one. If so, sophistic "wisdom" (70B) about virtue would be merely a verbal heightening of the content of the definition. But Meno is bound too closely to sophistic discourse to see this theoretical point. Hence his first two definitions break down without his realizing the import of the failure; moreover, he shows no impulse to remedy it. Thus the whole discourse is in jeopardy.

To overcome this, Socrates supplies model definitions, the first two being respectively, an experiential and a theoretic model (see chap. 2). These would be exhaustive if Meno were working from an interest in the subject, but he is captious about the first and unresponsive to the second (75B–76A).

The way Socrates handles this disengaged reaction of Meno sets, in miniature, the basic dramatic pattern of the dialogue. Socrates sees that he must relax his standard if he is to make contact. To stimulate a new definition of virtue from Meno, he gives, as he says, a poetic model in the style of Gorgias (76C). It appeals to Meno and rescues the discourse, but the *way* it appeals shows how slight the contact is. Meno does not respond to it as a suggestive guide for defining virtue but rather enjoys it and asks for more such definitions (77A). The limit of Socrates' adjustment to Meno here is indicated by his response: he says he cannot continue long in this style (77A).[27]

After prodding, Meno does use the model, taking a definition from "the poet's words" (77B). At this point, he has lost the possibility of seeing that Gorgias' type of poetry properly would embroider a definition, not provide one. Rather, the definition pleases him because it is poetic, so that when Socrates refutes it, Meno is discomfited and voices his dismay about the *aporia* which the torpedo fish has caused him to suffer (80A–B). Even so, he is not as seriously affected by the refutation as, say, Euthyphro is by the one he suffers in the dialogue bearing his name. Meno has no practical interest at stake in his encounter with Socrates; his intellectual interest seems to be in the technique of eloquence or eristic, not the nature of virtue. In any event, Meno's *aporia* here does not give him the kind of impulse which an *aporia* gives the slave-boy—to "push on gladly in the search" (84B).

The plot is thus almost at a standstill. Yet, though intellectually disengaged, Meno still wants some compensatory gratification for his discomfiture.[28] Socrates interprets Meno's torpedo-fish analogy as an effort by Meno to elicit a compliment in return from Socrates about his handsomeness (80C). Earlier Socrates had admitted that "spoilt beauties" hold a "despotic power" over him so long as their bloom is on them (76C). But now he refuses to pay Meno the hoped-for compliment. If he did pay it, the essential movement of the plot would be deflected. It is characteristic of Meno that he would substitute a personal (like a poetic) gratification for the recognition of an intellectual impulse. Socrates refuses to provide the substitute, suggesting instead a joint search for the definition. Meno, thereupon, not getting the hoped-for compliment responds with his famous paradox (see chap. 3), challenging Socrates and so reviving the exchange.

This thin thread of Meno's engagement in the discourse thus leads into the slave-boy episode as the answer to the paradox. For some time this episode appears to be succeeding in its purpose—to stimulate Meno to inquire into the *ti* question. Socrates' myth of recollection causes Meno to drop his contentious stance and to express a desire to be "taught" (shown) how knowledge is recollected rather than communicated from the outside. He then agrees that the demonstration with the slave-boy shows this, and thus Socrates can now confidently renew his proposal to search for a definition. Meno momentarily agrees, but at this point comes the peripety, for the proposal fails when Meno balks at it, asserting his preference for his original question. Socrates yields, making the peripety a double one. Not only does Meno's balking reverse the prospect of inquiry set up by the success of the slave-boy episode but Socrates' acquiescence reverses *his* own stand on the priority of the definitional inquiry as well. The reversal is nonetheless probable for logical-psychological reasons, as we shall set forth in chapters 4 and 8; but there are additional dramatic points about it to be noted here.

Given the newly discovered fact that if Meno is to be engaged, the topic must be the acquisition of virtue, parts I and II appear retrospectively to have been a detour between the opening question and the present return to it. There is nothing strange, dramatically, about detours, for example, Oedipus' suspicion of Teiresias and Creon, or Hamlet's many diversions from killing Claudius. But what is the function of this detour? It prepares Meno for discourse now which to some extent is a mutual undertaking without loss of the security of a master, for he has seen Socrates teach without teaching as it were. Although this is an advance from the rote study under Gorgias toward Socratic method, Meno does not want to run the risk of the novelty of a definition as unfamiliar to him as the diagonal was to the boy. And the detour has shown Socrates that he must adjust his priorities or otherwise modify his customary method if the exchange is to be fruitful for Meno. In showing Meno's limitations, it provides the reader as well as Socrates with a basis for deciding whether Socrates' later minimal success with Meno goes as far as possible in affecting him by discourse. We are reluctant to relegate the two most celebrated characteristically Socratic parts of the dialogue to this instrumental role and to assign a consummatory role to the "doxic" final part yet to come. But just as these roles, in fact, hold for logical structure, so do they for the dramatic. This interpretation need involve no disparagement of the earlier parts; to view Hamlet's killing of Claudius as the consummation of the plot is not to depreciate the dramatic and substantive value of Hamlet's delays.

Stages of Change in Meno II—Engagement. Although the subject matter is now determined to be what Meno wants, the acquisition of virtue, Meno is not engaged by that alone. The preceding failure shows that two conditions still have to be met if he is to be engaged. First, he is now prepared for a search, but it cannot depart very far from the authoritative format to which he is accustomed; an affirmative conclusion is needed. To exhibit a dialectical vista before an aristocratic disciple of Gorgias will not do; something definite and repeatable is wanted. The man who is troubled by the paradox of inquiry must know what he has come to know. Second, it is also clear that for this conclusion to have any significance for him, some sort of aporetic unsettling must precede it, rather than the merely verbal *aporia* of the earlier part. These conditions are gradually realized through a new Socratic strategy.

a) In beginning now with the hypothetical argument (86E ff.), Socrates employs a method which functions constructively to set the focus on cognitive sophistical questions, and yet still approaches the sophistic style to which Gorgias has accustomed Meno. If this is so, as we shall argue, then dramatically we now have an indulgence of Meno in method as well as in the question treated. That the constructive function is nonetheless Socratic is indicated by Socrates' statement that his use of the geometric example depends on Meno's relaxing his authority a bit (86E). But the drama of the episode consists in the fact that Socrates gives virtue a treatment as laudatory (and logically faulty) as anything Gorgias could produce. In the hypothetical argument Socrates works from the attachment of virtue to the word most useful in fine speeches (virtue is always "good"—87D); while he uses the profitable consequences of virtue as the point from which to make inferences about it, this treatment also eliminates any need for an internal analysis. The principal point is that to find virtue to be knowledge or wisdom (hence teachable) is the wholly laudatory thing to say, and to sing virtue's praises is undoubtedly the object in the fine speeches Gorgias prepared Meno to make. To construe the hypothetical deductive section dramatically in the way that we have—as saying what Meno finds most satisfying—is more plausible than to consider it the locus of Socrates' real opinion about virtue, since he subsequently upsets it. It should be noted that Meno is the one who actually draws the conclusion of the argument as a necessity (*anangkaion*—89C), while Socrates himself will not make the inference explicit. We have here an ironic twist on the drawing of answers from within the respondent, but a twist which nonetheless mirrors the way Socrates in dealing with the slave-boy had set up an opening for the boy's initial wrong answer.

The slave-boy's *aporia* had been productive because he had some reason to believe in the answers which were later overturned (that doubling the side would double the square). The dramatic problem in engaging Meno is similarly to reach an (overturntable) answer to which he will have some attachment. The deductive cogency of the hypothetical proof that virtue is knowledge is well adapted to provide such an answer. We recall the way in which Meno put the question to Socrates at the opening of the dialogue, offering several enumerated replies, any one of which might turn out to be satisfactory. If he saw it thus as a variable and disputable matter (allowing for a good display or debate), he could now see the apparent certainty of the new deductive Socratic argument as providing him with an irrefutable position: Virtue is brought to the peak of praise (teachable because it is "wisdom") in a way he thinks is "necessary." In this Socrates has exceeded Gorgias. Meno can now make a particularly fine speech to anyone who asks for one or challenges him. There is no reason to suppose that this is not still his main interest; the supposed fact that virtue is knowledge and teachable does not itself stimulate him to further thought. But the cogency of the proof is strong enough for him to be averse to the prospect of its being upset (89C–D); at the end of the section Meno is indeed surprised when Socrates opens up this prospect by expressing doubts about the conclusion of the argument, thus setting up the preaporetic feeling needed for a subsequent engagement. To see Socrates in this section as being careless because of his contempt for Meno misses the dramatic function of the demonstrative form of the argument in its process of engaging Meno.

b) The next step is to confirm Socrates' doubt about the hypothetical conclusion by refuting it in the Anytos episode, thereby producing a new analogue of *aporia* in Meno. The Anytos episode bases its counterclaim (virtue is not teachable) on the empirical fact that there are no teachers of virtue—virtue here being the everyday sort practiced in Athens and Thessaly. No doubt Socrates could have produced a deductive rather than an empirical argument that virtue is not teachable. But this would serve neither the logic nor the drama. The "necessity" which Meno had seen in the first deductive argument, that virtue is teachable, would have given way in his mind—rebutted by a counter-logic—so that he could again consider the question of acquisition a good one for debates, permitting answers as variable as the set of alternatives which had been initially set before Socrates. But because Socrates overturns the conclusion that virtue is teachable by empirical evidence (93A–94E) and by the confusion of the poets (95D–E), he raises perplexities. In our present terms the link now missing in Thessaly between the sphere of Gorgias' discourse or "wisdom" and the sphere of ongoing practices and values has been made; that is, the "wisdom" discourse is seen as making a substantive claim of the presence of teachers which ongoing practices belie. This empirical undercutting of what must have seemed a speechmaking treasure leads Meno to "wonder" (*thaumazein*) whether there are perhaps no good men at all or, if there are, how they come to be (96D). The problem for Meno is thus no longer verbal—he is finally engaged.

This wonder is an obvious analogue of technical *aporia*, but in one sense it marks more of an engagement than the slave-boy's numbness about the problem posed by Socrates. Here Meno himself has been the one to reformulate the problem, posing it in a more perplexing form than anything suggested by Socrates.

c) The momentum of his strategy leads next to an analogue—though in this case a faint one—of the recollection which has been alleged necessary for learning. Socrates responds to Meno's wonder by saying that they must look to themselves (96D). As with recollection, the internal process is opposed to being taught. Prodicus has not educated Socrates well, nor Gorgias Meno. Prodicus' failure, in spite of his fame for making distinctions, presumably "explains" Socrates' failure to distinguish knowledge and good opinion because of the identity of their effects. We may infer the nature of Gorgias' failure from Meno's habits and from Socrates' early description of Gorgias as handing down authoritative pronouncements. The fault of Gorgias' method here is that the disciple is supposed to be impressed without having a responsive chord struck within him. In contrast in the dialogue we soon have a response from within Meno that is evoked by Socrates, marking the final phase in Meno's engagement. It occurs when Socrates has convinced Meno that right opinion is as useful as knowledge and is always right (97C). Meno is then struck again by "wonder," this time over why knowledge should ever be more prized than right opinion (97D). At this point, Meno, on his own, makes the practical into the measure of the value of cognition and does this at the expense of the supposed superiority of knowledge to opinion. Although Socrates then restores knowledge to its place (98A), it is evident that for the moment he has overcome the separation of sophistic "knowledge" from Thessalian practices which he had encountered initially in Meno. Meno is now as ready as he will ever be for an affirmative finding of practical rather than mere sophistic value.

The Significance of the Change. In our earlier discussion of the end points of the plot we indicated the significance of Meno's being brought to the belief that virtue is inspired opinion. We are now in a position to discuss more adequately, though summarily, the change this marks in him, its value and its limitations.

Since the belief carries with it the denial that virtuous men are wise, Meno is accepting a view which thereby ranks virtue below the level at which sophistry would place it. There may be a sarcastic attitude toward "virtuous" leaders in Socrates' statement.[29] The important point, however, is that the denial of wisdom in virtue is explicit and is recognized by Meno to be a view offensive to Anytos. Meno's acceptance of it marks a clear change from his state of mind prior to the long preparation he has undergone.

The similarity of the leaders' inspiration to poetic processes (99D) puts them on ground which Gorgias has already made familiar to Meno and which he admires. There is a shift here too, this one positive as against the denial of wisdom mentioned above. Virtue is now not merely the subject matter of poetry and sophistry which Meno admires, but has become intensely poetic, as if it were itself a poem having its own content in thought and action.

Perhaps neither the negative nor the positive features of Meno's new belief are important theoretically, but they converge in a possible practical value. Since virtuous men are not wise there is at least room, and possibly need, for open discussion; but since denying their wisdom is not denying their inspired virtue, such discussion does not entail a disregard of their service to the state. The consequence of the new belief is thus anti-repressive: the plot accordingly ends with Socrates' encouraging Meno to persuade Anytos of this gentling belief for the good of the people of Athens.

Such an act by Meno would itself go beyond the shift from the concern with discourse as verbal to discourse as consequential. It would have a touch of altruism. Meno and the Thessalians are quite practical, as Socrates' opening remarks indicate. Sophistry for them is an idle luxury, not at the center of life as it is for Gorgias or Phaedrus. We have seen evidence that Meno's tendency, as in his momentary identification of virtue with wealth-getting and the like, is to follow conventional practices for the goods they can bring. It is an achievement for Socrates to implant in him, even fleetingly, the motive of talking with Anytos neither for display nor for personal benefit but for softening Anytos' attitude toward Socrates; and we may note next how this too has been set up by the *poion* section (pt. III).

Meno's initial feeling of discomfiture and the resultant eristic challenge he makes to Socrates come after the refutation of his definition in part I. At that point, another person in discourse was, for him, either a master or an opponent. In part III, however, though Socrates cannot go too far from the role of a Gorgian master, he also keeps close enough to his own criteria of inquiry for Meno himself to refer to the exchange as "our investigation" (96D). The attitude toward Socrates, built up in Meno by this process of guided give-and-take, makes the final "pro-Socratic" charge congenial to him, though his response is left unstated. Had Meno succeeded in the charge, then this might indeed have constituted a return trip of wisdom from Larisa to Athens. This ending is a final sign in support of our argument that part III is the culmination of the dialogue.

Socrates' role as protagonist supports this analysis as it comes to a head in the final section. His novel determination that knowledge and opinion are of comparable practical value and that virtue comes from the gods constitutes his final creative achievement. This takes him beyond the refutative categories, geometrical models, and existing public opinion which he previously depended upon. And this final insight is the culmination of the narrative.

The Dramatic Achievement. To help assess the achievement of the plot we will consider a fact which may seem to argue against the importance of the ending. Historically, Meno did not actually persuade Anytos; we do not even know whether he tried. It is known on the other hand, though not from Plato, that Meno went on to act corruptly and treacherously. Socrates brought him to the threshold of a single virtuous act but evidently without further result. Does this not show that nothing was achieved?

Our response depends in part on what alternative was open. We believe we have shown that, minimal as the effect was, it was more than one might have thought possible. Meno is as invulnerable or at least insensitive to defeat as he is unreceptive to educative dialectic. It is hard to imagine an interlocutor, fond of discourse and willing to talk, who would be more impervious to Socrates than is Meno. Much of the dialogue, as we have seen, involves a process in which Socrates learns that neither what seriously shakes others—refutations—nor what stimulates them—inquiry—takes hold of Meno. It is not far-fetched to think of Meno as a challenge to the arts of Socrates, for although in the *Republic* Socrates sets prerequisites for anyone to engage in dialectic, in Athens he would talk with whoever was willing. The slave-boy presents a similar case. He is a maximal challenge to Socrates' ability to guide a man to recollection. This is the reason— dramatically—why nearly all the adverse commentary on the logic of the slave-boy episode misses the point. So it is with the adverse commentary on the apparently ironic depreciation of virtue in part III. Only an argument of this sort can divert Meno from sophistry to consequences and from self-serving motives to the motive for a virtuous act.

The analogy between the slave-boy's and Meno's experiences with Socrates can be extended to the post-dialogue situation. Socrates says that the boy will come to know if the proper questions are asked of him (85C–D). But it is unlikely that anyone *will* ask. The paradox of *aporia* is that although its purpose is to lead one to see for oneself, it so numbs that one cannot do so without still more guidance. Such dependence exists also, but more extremely, in action. The point made about leaders is that they are good guides; the maintenance and exercise of public virtue in citizens depends upon them. The consent of citizens is required, but it is consent, not generative action. Socrates is only a momentary guide for Meno, whom he presents to Anytos in the dialogue as one seeking guidance (91A). Socrates prepares him to accept a charge and then formulates it for him. Meno's fondness for the praise of virtue and his complaisant lip-service to it—he does not know how to articulate, say, Calliclean principles—make him susceptible to Socrates' lead. Indeed, he is a test case of the presence in men of the operational dispositions susceptible to good guidance. But without a guide they are in action like the slave-boy in thought, and Meno will never have Socrates again. The importance of the freedom needed for the social cultivation and recognition of such guides is the point of the dialogue, to the logic of which we now turn.

2 Definition and Dialectic in the *Meno*

The opening section of the dialogue presents a search for the definition of virtue (70A–80B). Although defining a concept is fundamental to Plato in many of his writings, he nowhere precisely defines definition itself. Rather, he treats definition in so many diverse contexts, emphasizing in each a different aspect of it as central, that a general and literal account of "Plato's notion of definition" seems prima facie suspect.[1] The variations in treatment apply as much to the fundamental features of "definition" as they do to the concepts being defined (piety, justice, courage, etc.). In each case the argument develops a context within which the notion of definition as well as the term being defined acquire a rigorous structure and a particular significance. This contextual development constitutes minimally what we mean by Plato's definitional dialectic.

The context itself develops throughout the argument, which is given a circumstantial setting at the beginning of every dialogue. The setting in the *Meno* has been considered by many to be unusual, and is in fact specially adapted to the problem and method being developed in the dialogue.

(i)   *The Setting*

Referring to Meno's opening question on the acquisition of virtue, A. E. Taylor states that this beginning remark has "an abruptness hardly to be paralleled in the genuine work of Plato by the direct propounding of a theme for discussion; there are not even the ordinary formalities of salutation."[2] Taylor sees this deviation as evidence of the early date of composition of the *Meno*.[3] Hoerber notes specifically how unusual it is that the dialogue opens without description of locale, occasion, or participants.[4]

The opening should, however, be analyzed for its contrast with other dialogues rather than for the expected similarity to them. Although Meno's universal question is given no particularized scene, the social setting is strongly underscored. Socrates parries Meno's question with a description of Meno's Thessaly and his own Athens, both viewed in terms of the resources they offer for dealing with a question such as Meno's. Thessaly is characterized by its practical success and its new-found "wisdom." This success is in activities, wealth-getting and horsemanship, which, implicitly here and explicitly in later parts of the dialogue, appear to be in themselves morally indeterminate. "Wisdom" in Gorgian discourse is marked by giving answers to any question put by anyone. Such discourse of itself is not inquiry and Socrates can describe it here in terms of style without supposing that anyone participating in it has to come to grips with questions of virtue. He singles out for special mention the Aleuadae, whom Plato's contemporary reader would recognize as having sided with Xerxes against the Greeks. In brief, there is little virtue in practice but much talk about it. As for Athens, the practical situation is not indicated, though this will emerge in the Anytos episode and is suggested in the opening: The city suffers postwar stress, but there are and have been virtuous men in Athens. Athens once provided conditions for virtue in its citizens, yet the emphasis here, reflecting the recent changes, is on the present absence of "wisdom" about virtue; wisdom has traveled the road to Larisa, and Athenians are not disposed to discuss such questions as Meno's, at least not in the sophistic or "theoretic" manner in which he puts them.

The situations in Thessaly and Athens thus differ from each other in two ways. Discourse about virtue is available in the one but not in the other, and virtue is present primarily in the latter. Yet in neither city is there substantive, fruitful discussion of virtue: there is no connection between discourse and virtue—theory and practice. Socrates argues accordingly that any answer must be presented by Meno (and Gorgias) and that in view of Athens' condition the first question to be answered is the more basic, What is virtue? rather than that of virtue's acquisition.

We noted in chapter 1 the dramatic aspects of this shift to the definitional question. Here we note the consequences of this shift made by the commentary on Thessaly and Athens, for it reverses a common relation of setting to theme in Plato—that in which an individual scene, such as Socrates' impending execution, provides a concrete beginning from which to abstract a universal theme, such as the immortality of the soul. Conversely, the *Meno* gives social meaning to the universal question, how virtue is acquired, by generalizing it from the particularities of how virtue and discourse are related in specified, existent states; ultimately this becomes a question of how Athens has provided for continuity of leadership in her history. This reveals the operationalist character of the work. The localized scene usually supplied by Plato is missing, but the problem of the dialogue is presented by generalizing two situations that constitute the setting, that is, the minimal problem lies in exploring the social significance of sophistic lip-service to virtue where virtue itself is hardly to be found, as in Thessaly, and of the distrust of virtue, where, as in Athens to some extent, virtue persists but is unknown.

The immediate effect of locating themes in the social context is to enlarge the extent to which the means for resolving moral difficulties (mainly here impediments to discourse) are sought in its existent features. An obvious and striking sign of this is found in the criterion set up here for judging Meno's forthcoming definitions of virtue. Nominally the criterion is the same as that of the *Apology* —Socratic ignorance. But in the *Meno* this means the opposite of what it means in the *Apology*; that is, here Socratic ignorance is the same as the state of mind of any Athenian on virtue—tied to their present loss of great wisdom.

Plato often notes the difficulties impeding discourse in ordinary sociopolitical situations. What is peculiar in the *Meno* is that he never wholly turns away from everyday affairs. The *Republic* furnishes the best example of this turning away as it exhibits virtue as knowable. Even in the *Apology*, where Socrates talks of Athens as she is, he finds a lack of idealism and prescribes a total reordering of the hierarchy of values. The broad problems with which the *Meno* begins are how to make ongoing discourse relevant (Thessaly) and how to bring existent virtue into men's cognitive ken (Athens). Moreover, the lines of solution to these problems are sought within the limits of the resources provided by the circumstantial situations. The development of the dialogue shows this, for Socrates eventually presents the Athenian leaders as paradigms of virtue and emphasizes generally the profitability of virtue. Finally, the conclusion that virtue is a gift of the gods makes plausible both the unqualified sophistic praise of it and the distrust of theoretically precise prescriptions for virtuous action.

The importance given the setting as the available moral resource and as the locus of the problem, indicates that something other than the *ti*-form discussion is needed to meet the problem as prefigured in the opening. But the inadequacy of the *ti* question must first be shown, and shown in such a way that the initially rejected topic of acquisition is seen finally as significant for an exchange between the two men. The first argument of the dialogue—about the definitions, accomplishes both.

(ii)   *The Special Way the Definition of Virtue is Sought*

The *Meno's* special definitional approach can be seen a) in contrast to two other Platonic dialogues and b) in the preliminary remarks which set its definitional problems.

a) The *Meno* is usually compared with the *Protagoras* because both are concerned with the teachability (or acquirability) of virtue and whether it is one or many. Yet they differ significantly in the treatment of these problems.

The *Protagoras* never rises to the level of a search for the definition of virtue; rather, its frame assumes man can never *be* good but can only *become* good under pressing circumstances and can remain good until overcome by such circumstances (339–48). The teacher of virtue helps men become and remain somewhat better.[5] In the *Protagoras*, Socrates, looking to the wisest old man in Greece as a model, therefore concentrates upon the question of the unity of virtue, not on what it is. By contrast the *Meno*, in which Socrates himself is old and is warned about his possible difficulties with the state, uses the unity of virtue to guide the search for a definition; this then introduces the central problem of how man acquires virtue. Neither dialogue identifies virtue with wisdom, though in both the notion of virtue is closely related to a cognitive function. In the *Protagoras*, man's good or virtue is determined by his calculative or measuring capacity in maximizing his pleasures and minimizing his pains (where miscalculation is possible owing to distance in time of prospective pleasures and pains). One of the problems throughout the dialogue is the reciprocal measuring of each man (Socrates and Protagoras) against the other when no man eminent enough to judge between them is available. In the *Meno*, the cognitive function is right opinion contrasted with knowledge as the standard. Thus the *Protagoras* does not even begin the search for a definition whereas in the *Meno* the search for an internal structure of virtue lays the ground for an inquiry into its acquirability.

In the *Euthyphro*, a definition of piety is sought within a setting of a son's duty to his father, the young to the old, the inferior to the superior—the virtue itself embodying the relationship. Socrates conducts the search by attempting to establish what is subsumed under piety, what is equivalent to it, and what it is subsumed under in turn, namely, justice. The *Meno*, on the other hand, asks abruptly how virtue comes to man as a question about the way two diverse things become joined (70A). This question of joining two things is immediately turned into the question of our knowing one of the things (71A–B)—this cognitive question *itself* presumably being a kind of joining. Socrates thus argues that one must know virtue before one can determine its properties, for example, how it is acquired.

In contrast with the *Protagoras*, then, the *Meno* emphasizes the internal structure of virtue in its search for a definition; in contrast with the *Euthyphro*, it seeks to determine not the relations of the terms to subordinate and superordinate concepts, but rather the contact or joining of two things, man and virtue.

b) This is borne out by the special way the *Meno* raises the definitional question. One might suppose that a man may know many properties of a thing without having determined what the thing is. Plato would allow, of course, that we may have opinions about things without knowing them. What does Plato mean by "knowing what virtue is"? In point of fact, he gives us the key in two steps in this introduction to the search for a definition: 1) if one does not know what virtue is then one does not know the thing virtue at all or in any way (*to parapan*—71A–B) and 2) not knowing virtue at all corresponds by analogy to not knowing Meno and therefore not knowing Meno's individual properties.[6] These steps indicate two aspects of knowing what virtue is.

First, if we know anything about virtue, then we know something about what it is. This makes a mere truism of the point that we must first know what virtue is before we can know its properties. But knowing what it is includes knowing its properties as *parts* of what it is—this is the inclusive sense of the term "definition." This sense internalizes the total content of a concept such as virtue in contrast to a definition which draws out a part of a whole as an "essence" of some sort.

Second, virtue, in being analogized to Meno, is treated as a particular entity which can be known only by direct acquaintance (*gignōskein*—70B). The use of the analogy of virtue to Meno thus gives a special twist to the problem of definition as found here. This twist— the knowing of the particular—gives the *Meno* its distinctly contemporary quality despite the conventional view of Platonic knowledge as always of the universal. The use of the notion of acquaintance (not unlike Bertrand Russell's) helps to focus on virtue as a particular with its total internal content. This transforms what appeared to be palpably untrue (that we must know what a thing is before we can know its properties, that is, how it is acquired) into a special kind of problem: that of knowing by acquaintance.

These two points emphasize the existential character of the particular to be known, on the one hand, and, on the other, set the minimal requirement that such knowledge be of things with which we have at least some slight contact. Further, Athenians are unacquainted with virtue, and Socrates, living in such a world, claims he has not known or been directly acquainted with any men who know what virtue is. Socrates states this in spite of the fact that he has been acquainted with Gorgias, who, Meno believes, does know what virtue is and has told Meno what it is. Meno is thus in the position to convey directly to Socrates what he, Meno, has accepted as knowledge acquired from Gorgias. In summary, then, the *Meno* derives its special approach to the problems examined from an emphasis on knowing a particular object and its internal structure through direct acquaintance.

(iii)   *Definitions of Virtue*

Meno makes three attempts to define virtue (71E–72A, 73C–D, and 77B). Each attempt is examined, criticized, and discarded, though each adds a facet to the total effort. Socrates criticizes each for introducing a multeity whereas an adequate definition presumes a unity. The multeity in each case is differently constituted and adapted to the character of the notion offered as a definition. In addition, Socrates offers Meno three model definitions as examples.

All this suggests a number of formalistic questions which may serve as means for eliciting the content of this argument. For example, why are there three major attempts at definition rather than two or four—or ten? What accounts for the sequence of definitions, and how does one effort and its refutation lead in a definite fashion to the next? Why are model definitions included and why do they consist as they do, that is, two of "figure" and one of "color" rather than three attempts to define either "figure" or "color"? How are the model definitions related to the attempted definitions of "virtue"? In short, what is the rationale of the total scheme? Such questions suggest that an interpretive concentration solely upon a single argument treated in isolation is insufficient and misleading,[7] and that details must be examined in light of the total structure of the argument.

The search for a definition (71E–79E) breaks into four clearly distinguishable parts: the first attempt (71E–73C), the second attempt (73D–75A), the model definitions (75B–76E), and the final attempt (77B–79E). In the first attempt, Socrates assumes the singularity of human virtue, while Meno suggests it is different for various kinds of people at different stages of life and in different circumstances. Meno finds unconvincing Socrates' analogy of virtue to the singularity of kinds of things (bees) or of properties (health and strength), though he agrees reluctantly when Socrates suggests that diverse actions done in the *same way* indicate an identity of reference for "human virtue." Meno's position can be interpreted as an expression of the ancient sophistical (and twentieth-century) belief that man has no essence and therefore no unique excellence, but acts existentially from moment to moment, with no human or divine standard of excellence to guide him. The Socratic argument raises the possibility of the existence of virtue as an identifiable property of human beings, manifested in their actions and distinct from the varied circumstances of different people.

Meno's second attempt at definition (ability to govern men) is based on action peculiarly appropriate to men as they achieve their excellence in political communities. Socrates notes that this is apparently not applicable to all men (children, slaves), and thus lacks the existential universality defended in the first attempt at definition. One might suppose that the definition signifies the unity of power and wisdom (*Republic* V) so necessary for successful rule directed to the good of the ruled as a community. However, Socrates presumes, and Meno accepts, the notion that the capacity to rule may be divorced from human virtue, so that the differentia "justly" must be added to yield "ability to govern justly." And this addition does not take for granted the inclusive role which justice plays in the *Republic*, but rather suggests that it is merely one of many virtues. The multeity suggested here is not that of a lack of identity, but rather a lack of generic unity, allowing diverse species-oriented definitions. Clearly, this effort at definition is designed to raise the logical question about the proper structure of any definition as inherent in such attempts at abstract formulations.

We note here Meno's third definition of virtue (desire for and ability to procure fine things) as the completion of the structure of definitions of virtue, reached only after the examination of the model definitions of figure and color. The inclusion of "desiring good things" and the subsequent purging of this portion of the definition (because it is applicable to everyone, even to evil men) reinforces the existential orientation of the definition to human actors. Certainly the definition is concentrated on the objects procured. The formal criticism that "procuring goods" be done "justly" or by means of a bit of virtue, emphasizes another sense of multeity distinct from that of mere otherness and of multiple species—namely, that of parts within a whole. Apparently, two schemata are operating in the movement through these three definitions: 1) The substantive schema involves three closely related factors, though it concentrates on one in each case. The factors are the agents (human roles), the acting (or ability to act), and the object of action. 2) The formal schema involves the three senses of the singleness of virtue: the one over many—identity, one genus as distinct from many species, the wholeness as contrasted with many bits or parts.

This schema takes on added significance in light of the model definitions, which in fact model the structural relations of the definitions of virtue themselves. Socrates introduces the model definitions to clarify the species-genus relation of justice-virtue, using the round—or straight—figure relation as another example. By indicating the necessity for finding what is common to all virtue, Socrates defines figure (75B–D, 75D–76A) and color (76A–D).

The first definition states that figure always follows color, thus stating the universal existential concomitance of figure with color. This combination of a universal and an existential character undercuts attempts to separate analytic, necessary, and universal (vacuous) relations, on the one hand, from synthetic, contingent, and existential facts, on the other. Further, it provides anyone, who knows when he is looking at a color, with a purchase on figure—provides, that is, with the opinion that he in some way is encountering figure. Now when Meno objects that one could say one did not know what color is, Meno is applying an impossible formal criterion (no undefined terms in a definition), as Socrates had done with Meno's definitions of virtue. Socrates, however, treats Meno's objections as eristic, since in fact the definition of color given later (76D) would not help one use this definition of figure as a starting point for inquiry. The definition requires that its user have the power to abstract from the sense perception of colors the boundaries demarcating them. This would give one "forms" (shapes), but forms still universally attached to the concrete datum. The trouble with the definition is that it is made for an eristic antagonist; that is, it is true and defensible against him rather than true and mutually understood (75D). What Meno needs, and apparently lacks, is not a definition of color but rather knowledge of how to pass from familiar color-sensing to shapes as their universal concomitant. (The first definition of virtue fails to provide even the opportunity for such a move, since the fact that there is a virtue peculiar to man does not mean that this virtue accompanies every man.)

The second definition of figure as the limit of a solid clearly does not establish a universal existential tie, but rather turns on the intrinsic conceptual relations of the genus-differentia-species type. Meno could ask for further enlightenment about the term "solid," but he does not. This definition is conceptually most satisfactory because it reflects in this intrinsic relation (limiting, bounding) the task of definition itself as a search for boundaries of terms. Moreover, it is a friendly one, using terms understood by the respondent; it contains a virtually built-in potential for theoretical or geometrical development. By contrast with the genus-species difficulty of the second definition of virtue, with its uncertainty whether "just rule" was a kind of rule, the second definition of figure makes it immediately evident that "red figure," for example, is not a species of figure. Meno does not object to this definition but rejects it as a pattern, asking instead for a definition of color. Meno could not formulate these relationships, certainly not all of them, but his responses are understandable as intuitive reactions of one whose attraction to Gorgias' sophistic rests so much on its suitability to his rote memory. As many persons have noted, the name "Meno" derives from the root for memory.

He had thus rejected the first definition on formal grounds; he requires some sense of system, being unable to proceed simply from the universal conditions in familiar experience or direct acquaintance with the object. The second definition provides a clear basis for a determinate system, but it clearly leads into geometry and away from the familiar. When Meno asks for the definition of color instead of figure he is in effect asking for a system within and about a sensible, familiar object. The thing in question is already known by direct acquaintance; what Meno desires is to be shown how its coming about involves a unified system.

The definition of color befits Meno's fondness for Empedoclean physicalistic constructions and Gorgian poetic style (*tragikē*—76E), but it is inferior for Socrates. The definition involves a system of operations constituting antecedent conditions for seeing a color. The system purports to show why color is what always follows shapes of a certain sort; that is, color, as an effluence of form commensurate with sight, and sensible, is seen whenever the shape of the effluence is commensurate with the pores of the eye. This systematic structure "explains" the direct acquaintance with the object (color). And the definition completes the cumulative pattern of relationships of figure and color implicit in the first and second definitions of figure. The first defines figure in terms of color, and the second is completely independent of the notion of color. But finally, the definition of color is based on figured effluences emanating from bodies and adapted to enter the eye. (This definition is akin to the construction of material necessities in the *Timaeus*, where physical bodies are composed of bounded elements consisting of different elementary triangles, the elements accounting physically for such biological operations as sense functions.)

However, Socrates' reservations about this definition of color suggest that he finds this reductive physicalistic treatment theoretically unsatisfactory. Minimally, it assumes a thesis of the identity of mind and body. This would raise many further questions.

These model definitions parallel those of virtue, the three definitions in each case moving from the existential particular through the abstract theoretic to a comprehensive system of parts in a whole. The models treat purely cognitive problems, which are theoretically achievable, as distinct from the more inaccessible practical problem of virtue. In the *Republic* VI–VII, the practical is subsumed under the theoretic. Here, however, the theoretical model definitions, placed as they are between the second and third attempts to define virtue, serve as a bridge to the third definition of virtue. For the third definition, as we noted, turns on the proper (with justice) acquisition (procuring) of objects (wealth, etc.), just as the third model definition of color turned on the fitness of the eye for receiving emanations from bodies seen. The model definitions thus move the argument back to the notion of acquiring. Acquiring is an intrinsic part of what virtue is. The original question about the acquisition of virtue gave way to the question of what virtue is, and this in turn is found to involve the "proper" acquisition or non-acquisition of goods.

If virtue is to be treated in its familiar common forms (Meno felt that it is easy to say what it is), and is to be given some kind of systematic base, then the process of acquisition provides a frame. Although these definitions do not explicitly specify the significance of the "acquisition," they suggest its peculiar adaptation to a concern for finding order (some sort of "one") within the structure of continuing social practices.

The key question is, What is this "one"? As we have noted, Socrates calls it a whole rather than a genus or identity. As here presented it is not a whole in the sense of the organic unity of an animal with which the *Phaedrus* identifies a dialectician's speech (246C), nor is it a structure of functions such as the *Republic* IV sets up, nor even the unity of a harmony which the *Gorgias* ascribes to the soul as a basis for politics. But it also is not reducible to the bare totality of its ingredients. Rather, the whole here forms the basis for the indefinite persistence or recurrence of the objects. This involves an internal analysis not of the objects but of the system which provides the conditions for their repeatability.

What Socrates does with Meno's third definition of virtue shows that the same sense of whole applies here. First he rejects the desire for the good as part of the definition; because it exists in people who are not virtuous, it cannot be strictly commensurate with the modes of acquiring goods. Again, the way in which he calls for the whole follows the same model. Justice, temperance, and so forth, are the parts, but the whole he seeks is not to be got by adding up these parts in an exhaustive list, just as it is not to be got in the case of color were he to seek an enumeration of the different shapes which the color effluences have. Rather, the whole is in any of the parts, namely, in whatever there is about it which provides or constitutes the conditions of its repeated operation.

Obviously, the problem of acquisition is adapted to this other problem of the durability or continuation of virtue in a society. This property—an existential generalization—corresponds to the universal in strictly theoretic subjects. It is an important problem, and one which best suits Meno's capacities, the first two definitions having taken the measure as it were of his remoteness from substantive inquiry. As the first model definition shows, his sophistic background renders him incapable of proceeding without some sort of schematic context. The second shows Meno's desire to incorporate a schema at the level of familiar experience rather than at the merely theoretic level. The third locates the real problem for inquiry which exists within these limitations, and, as we have seen, acquisition is at the center of the inquiry. The theoretical model-definitions within the tripartite dialectic of definitions suggests the necessity for a theoretical inquiry about the acquisition of knowledge—the slave-boy episode. This episode then, prepares for "discovering" the solution to the existential practical problem of the acquisition of human excellence.

In summary, this account of the definitional section turns on the basic dichotomies (other-same, species-genus, part-whole) as they merge (many-one) and generate trichotomies in the step-by-step movement of the argument, the third step being a combination or synthesis of the two earlier steps (see Appendix, sec. 1). This dialectical building-up is further reinforced by the pattern of the model definitions, which also provide the transition for a return in the third attempt to define virtue, to the existential level of the first attempt. This interpretation yields intelligible answers to the formalistic questions raised at the beginning of this section about not only the number and content of the definitions but also about the relations between the attempts to define virtue and the unchallenged definitions of figure and color. We agree with Richard Robinson that Plato does expose eristic errors in the definitional section. However, our interpretation of the section clarifies more fully the type of errors Plato chooses for examination and the way faulty attempts at definition contribute to an enlarged pattern of thought. To emphasize mere "logical" errors in the failure to achieve an adequate definition is to treat the arguments too literally and to miss their special significance in the total context.

(iv)   *Definitional Dialectic*

We have argued that the unity and uniqueness of the definitional section combine a synoptic logical structure with a cumulative psychological process for Meno (see chap. 1). The content and form are mutually supportive. In this section we first use this unified structure as an example from which we attempt to build an expanded notion of Plato's definitional dialectic. In so doing, we introduce general considerations about other dialogues and about the overall nature of Plato's dialectic. Further, we attempt to clarify Plato's dialectic through contrast with other dialectics in the history of philosophy. Second, using this enlarged perspective, we view prospectively the entire dialogue in order to show that the definitional section achieves its purpose of determining the subject matter and appropriate method of the dialogue (also see Appendix, sec. i).

Definitions in Plato's Dialectic. It is generally recognized that Plato's concern for definitions and defining terms pervades the dialogues. This feature is obvious in the repetition of the attempts at definition in several of the earlier dialogues (*Republic* I, *Laches*, *Lysis*, *Euthyphro*) as they move through three identifiable stages and in some of the later dialogues (*Sophist*, *Statesman*). Further, there are many positive definitions in the dialogues, from the model definitions in the *Meno* to the definitions of the soul and love in the *Phaedrus*. In some cases, definitions serve as beginning-points for inquiry, in others as conclusions or summations. Some are explicit; some are implicit in a developing argument.

This pervasiveness of definitions and attempted definitions has led some commentators to attempt to formulate a general account of Plato's notion of definition (and of elenchus), that is, to create a "form" of definition for Plato.[8] Such an effort generally involves the promotion of one particular account of definition at the expense of other accounts in other dialogues which are treated as earlier immature anticipations or later aberrations. The selection of a given conception of definition as central and the concomitant narrowing of diversity through appeals to historical or accidental circumstances neglects the significance of each specific inquiry and the crucial important differences in subject matter and method appropriate to each such inquiry. Without question, however, the pervasiveness of definitions and definitional attempts in the dialogues suggests that, for Plato, definitions of terms constitute the end points of inquiries. Such definitions, when achieved, are our understanding of diverse aspects of that which is.

The subject matter of each inquiry is not some fixed literal area independent of the mode of inquiry into it. For example, though we might be inclined to identify the subject matter of the *Republic*, the *Statesman*, and the *Laws*, namely, as political philosophy, for Plato, the subject matters are quite diverse—each being determined by the method used to pose the problem. It is insufficient to distinguish these dialogues in some rough way as concerned with diverse aspects of man in his community—as concerned, for example, with the ideal possibilities in the nature of man seeking the best way of life, or with the kingly art of distinguishing the important diversities in human temperaments and realizing the political necessities of combining them in the right proportion, or with the limitations of circumstances (geographic, ethnic, etc.) of which lawgivers must take account in constructing a viable and stable polity. Using such a treatment, one might hold that the *Meno* is concerned with the existent actualities of daily life in which adjustment to changing situations is necessary. In this way, one might argue that these dialogues deal with identifiable species or parts of political philosophy as a genus or whole. But such a conclusion assumes a literally identifiable subject matter and a pre-determined system of classification.

Though such distinctions in the subject matter of the dialogues may seem suggestive, for Plato, there is no prior underlying system of classification. Rather, each dialogue generates its own classification of terms, as we have already seen in the definitional section of the *Meno*. And clearly the definition in the *Statesman* by the method of division generates a host of apparently *ad hoc* classifications, which Plato treats as most pertinent to the task of that dialogue.

From our synoptic view of the definitional section of the *Meno* emerges the notion that the *ti-poion* distinction functions in two different but important ways. The first and the commonly recognized way is that, in defining a thing such as virtue, one wishes to specify what that thing is, not merely some quality of the thing being defined. The second effect of the distinction is to produce a synoptic build-up of significance, turning on and refining the subject matter of the dialogue as being not what virtue is, but what the quality of man's acquiring virtue is. In this case the *ti* question is directed to the *poion* question about man's acquiring virtue, that is, man's acquiring virtue as a quality is what is under examination in the dialogue. A similar *ti-poion* inquiry is undertaken in the *Sophist* where the subject examined involves a mixture of that which is and that which is not. Other dialogues use different ordering questions appropriate pre-sumably for their particular subject matters. Thus, the *Laches* and *Theaetetus* examine courage and knowledge within a *ti-pōs* (in what manner) structure; the question of knowledge in the latter dialogue is pursued as Theaetetus and Socrates both give examples of various manners of knowing, from knowing arts (shoemaking) to knowing the nature of clay to knowing irrational lengths to knowing as a process of midwifing an idea. Or again, the *Philebus* and *Statesman* examine the good for man and the statesman within a *ti-poson* (or how much or of what measure) line of inquiry. For instance, the method of division used to identify the statesman begins with the assumption that he has knowledge and is designed to determine what his science is. The science is ultimately determined to be the appropriate measuring and proper mixing of the contrary virtues (courage and self-restraint) of the citizenry in actions undertaken to preserve the community. The determination that the statesman has knowledge is directly opposed to the *Meno*'s determination that political leaders act on the basis only of right opinion. But this is merely one of the numerous "conflicting" remarks within Plato's dialogues, and the conflict suggests that the meanings of "knowledge" in the two dialogues and in others, for example the *Theaetetus* and *Sophist*, may be quite different, in ways appropriate to the organization and subject matter of each.[9]

Thus, "knowledge" is conceived in terms of "acquaintance" in the *Meno*, construed in various complementary manners in the *Theaetetus* (no single construction being completely adequate), expressed in statements about the existence of nonbeing as well as being of combinations of concepts in the *Sophist*, and bound up with the standard of the mean fitting the circumstances and problems of command in the *Statesman*. Every such conception of knowledge is complete within a total context from which it is derived and in which its significance is illuminated: man's acquisitions, his eliciting (by questions or perception) and testing (by seeking and finding a rational account) to separate the true (*alēthēs*) from a mere image (*eidōlon*), his combining and separating of names to express changing states of affairs, his possession and exercise of the theory for maintaining and using the proper mix of human virtues necessary for a good society.

No overall entity or concept attaches to the conjunction of dialogues, except that of eliciting definitions appropriate to organizing the subject matter under examination. In each dialogue, however, a complete philosophic structure suited to the subject matter is erected. For example, in defining the statesman, the story of the world as involving cycles of time-reversals reinforces his role as knowing commander of the human community.

Plato's dialectic thus is not based upon rigidities or substantized ideal Forms, though these appear at various points in his analysis of problems, for example, in his treatment of ideal ways of life as in the *Republic* or in his argument for the immortality of the soul in the *Phaedo* where absolutely opposite forms are introduced in order to identify the soul as the principle of life which cannot admit of death. These forms do not provide the principles for unifying his thought, as important as they are in various ways for solving specified problems under consideration. Consequently there is no reason to appeal to linguistic and historical orderings of the dialogues or to dramatic devices to account for arguments that do not fit the pattern of a substantized system of forms.

What emerges is not a substantive or conceptual unity, but a *methodological* unity for Plato's definitional dialectic. A basic method with indefinite variations appropriate to problems and circumstances provides a flexible, comprehensive, and consistent unity adequate for an analysis of an unlimited diversity of concepts basic to human life and all that is.

This nondoctrinal dialectic with methodological unity contrasts sharply with diverse dialectics formulated throughout the history of philosophy; for examples, the dialectics of motion and rest (Heraclitus and Parmenides), of being (Plotinus), of faith (Augustine), of spirit (Hegel), of production-methods (Marx), of experience (Bradley), of process (Whitehead). Plato's dialectic takes place in the minds of men on given problems under specified circumstances. Though a given concept is central in one dialogue, it may be merely derivative in another. For example, the notion of acquisition, which is the subject matter of the *Meno*, appears in the *Republic* (337, 443–45, 451, 514, 618) in ways appropriate to an inquiry into ideal form. Or again, the concept of oneness, involving singularity and unity which is so essential for any definitional attempt (see secs. ii and iii above), is examined in Plato's *Parmenides* within a logico-metaphysical dialectic of being and not-being and of appearing to be and not-appearing to be.

Definitional Dialectic of Acquisition of the Meno. The subject matter of the *Meno* is man's acquisition of virtue. We use the word *acquire* throughout our discussion as a generic term for several words which Plato uses in different contexts. The problem of man's becoming virtuous is that of how virtue comes to him (*paragignetai*—70A); how the goods he seeks are procured (*porizomena*—77B–79E or *ktēta*—78C), how knowledge as something recollected is originally (as before birth) grasped or taken (*lambanomena*—85D) and then (in life) taken up (*analambanomena*—85D). Knowledge and true opinion, alike considered as not endowed by nature, are gained or added (*epiktēta*—98D). The word *acquire* provides the connections for these terms which mark the diverse kinds of acquisition. Both the diversity and unity of the terms are necessary to give sense to the unity and diversity within the dialogue.

The definitional section of the *Meno* thus presents a cumulative progression using both the substance and the criticism of what is apparently rejected. This is accomplished as the argument moves from an existential phase, through a theoretical phase, to a systematic structure of parts within a whole. One notion does not replace another, less adequate, notion. Rather, a synoptic structure is achieved which provides a general outline of the problem and establishes the subject matter of the dialogue: acquisition. This serves as the first stage of a three-part argument of which the primary structural feature is bracketing, not in the Husserlian sense of withdrawal to a more fundamental phenomenological level of analysis, but in the sense of a mathematical approximative technique—so essential when more exact procedures do not fit the problem at hand. The definitional section constitutes the first stage at which the attempt to define virtue is unsuccessful, though the tie between virtue and its acquisition is established. The third definitional attempt is itself reached by approximation and prefigures the dialogue's three-part bracketing structure (see chap. 8, sec. ii). Within this context Plato constructs the existential and theoretical organization for confronting the existential problem of action and the acquisition of the principles of action. What emerges is insight into the sociohistorical continuity of society, the related appropriate mode of philosophizing, and the implications of these for a theology.

3   The Slave-Boy Episode

The argument of the previous chapter suggests that even if an adequate definition of virtue cannot be found, the notion of man's acquisition of goods is the subject matter of the dialogue. The failure, however, to acquire such an adequate definition itself raises the question of the very acquirability of any knowledge as a good. Meno poses the relevant paradox, later restated by Socrates as follows: "A man cannot inquire about what he knows, because he knows it, and in that case he is in no need of inquiry, nor again can he inquire about what he does not know, since he does not know what he is to inquire" (80E).[1] The present chapter examines the resolution of this question as presented in the celebrated slave-boy episode.

(i)   *The Setting for the Slave-Boy Episode*

Socrates' answer to the paradox is that "knowledge is recollection." This thesis allows a man to have ideas of which he later becomes conscious by recollection; thereby overcoming the sharp division between not-knowing and knowing, and justifying inquiry. Socrates

35

initially sets up the thesis through a myth drawn from priests and poets "establishing man's power to recollect." The soul, being immortal, has learned all things (*chrēmata*—suggestive of acquirable things); since the things are related ("all nature is akin"—81D), the soul by remembering one thing is able to discover others by means of the connections. Socrates uses this myth chiefly to motivate inquiry, contrasting the courage to do so with indolence. Acting on trust in the promise of discovery thus becomes genuine action since, as we stated, the alternative is mere idleness.

Taken in its theoretical features the myth provides a direction of search without predetermining an inferential scheme. The objects of inquiry—all nature—are presented as discrete entities. The problem is to reestablish their connections, but the kind of connection is itself left open. The soul simply uses its knowledge of one thing to raise questions and seek for a connection with another. The slave-boy exchange illustrates the most integral kind of connection to be made in this nonhierarchical, nondialectical, open-ended search. This emphasis on the act of *dis*covering rather than on *re*covering knowledge of a definite kind and by a definite method, is mirrored both in the myth and in the conception of the soul in its earthly state as having learned, as if, to stretch a point, the soul's original knowledge and the discovery of it are identical. But our immediate point is that the present exchange between Socrates and Meno provides grounds for engaging in inquiry as a fundamental activity, but does so without preformalizing the reasoning process.

(ii)   *The Argument*

The showing (*endeixai* or *epideixaisthai*—82A–B) in the *Meno* that learning is "recovering by oneself knowledge within oneself" (85D6–7) has received much attention, from the time of Aristotle[2] to the present. Current interpretations[3] raise many diverse issues: whether the argument depends too much on empirical grounds such as drawings in the sand,[4] whether it is purely rational,[5] whether it proves the soul's existence before birth and reincarnation as well as the theory of forms,[6] whether the geometrical illustration is cogent mathematics or constitutes a criticism of the then prevailing state of geometrical knowledge,[7] whether the very shape of the argument itself is adequate to what it seeks to achieve, and so forth. An assumption of most current interpretations, which underlies the generation of such diverse issues, is the notion that knowledge is some duly constituted, formally ordered, discursive structure of ideas.[8]

If, however, the opening argument of the *Meno* (chap. 2, ii) provides the key to the use of the term *knowledge*, the more fundamental notion of it is that of direct acquaintance between the knower and the object known. If this is the case, then "knowing" is "becoming acquainted," or "learning," or "recollecting," or "discovering," or "having become acquainted." In this context the movement of ideas begins from acquaintance knowledge and progresses through an extension by description to the desired outcome, new acquaintance knowledge or discovery. The episode itself is presented in three distinct parts (82B–82E2, 82E12–84A, 84D–85B).[9] At the end of each part, Socrates and Meno review the state of the problem and of the slave-boy's state of mind about it.

Part A: Identification of the Subject Matter and Problem. Socrates' first question of the boy is, "Does he know [*gignōskein*—82B] that a square is a figure like this?" where the knowledge consists not of knowing the word *square* but of its use to denote a four-equi-sided, equi-middle-line figure of unspecified size. No mention is made of the assumption of four-equi-angles (held throughout). The question of size is then introduced, apparently by using the two middle lines to indicate a square with two-foot sides, containing four square feet. At this point, Socrates poses the double-square problem—how long will the side of a square be which contains twice the area of the given square?

Two questions arise at this point. First, why specify the size of the square when one can ask and answer correctly the question about constructing a double square independently of specifying size in standard units? In fact the answer ultimately reached is first presented in the more general form and then applied to the specified standard unit of the two-footed side square. Second, why specify a square on a side of two-feet rather than a unit (one-foot) square? As for the first, only those who already know the answer can construct a double square without reference to a standard size. Undoubtedly, the question involves the notion of relative size of one square to the other and one side length to the other. All notions of size are basically relative, though the notion of a standard relative size of a foot is itself based upon an arbitrarily selected unit as the unit of measurement. The use of a definite size provides the condition for testing whether suggested answers are correct. And this is a test of both the state of mind of the inquirer and of the whole notion of relative size—standard and neo-standard. Both are essential for the process of discovery.

As for the second question, there is one answer appropriate to the statement of the problem and a second appropriate to the first attempt to solve the problem (see pt. B below). First then, the square of a two-foot line contains within itself the substance of the problem in two senses. a) Viewed not in terms of doubling, but in terms of the difference in size between the one-foot square and the four-square-foot square produced by a two-foot side square, the original figure clearly makes obvious the faultiness of the boy's first suggested solution. Any highly observant boy would have noticed this and answered differently. This incident marks our boy as not precocious, raises the question of the rationale of his first suggested solution, and allows the process of discovery to proceed. b) The original figure contains in miniature the essence of the figure which provides the framework for solving the problem, of four smaller squares—this figure being constructed at the beginning of part C (see below).

Part B: The Boy's Rational Descriptive Extensions. Furthermore, the second reason for the use of the two-foot length of the side is that it allows for developing the argument through two stages in which the consequences of the suggested solutions can be grasped readily through the use of integers. These integers are applied to areas in a way not possible if a one-foot square were used. Finally, the two-foot side provides just the break in length which allows the argument to develop to a point where it is clear not merely that the answers given by the boy are incorrect, but that the very method he uses in attempting to give answers is unsatisfactory.

It is important to note the ostensible rationality of the boy's suggested solution. He suggests first that doubling the area must require doubling the side. When he sees that this fails, the results having given twice the area sought, he suggests that they add half as much to the side he had suggested originally. And the two-foot length of the side makes it easy to halve his original answer and to recognize that the consequence, the area of nine square units, is not the required one of eight square units. His ready routine ("to double, take twice as much"; "to halve, cut in two") and reasonable suggestions produce a total impasse. He, too, is numbed as if by a torpedo fish. The rational method is brought into question.

The slave-boy is brought to this same state of numbness (*narkē*)—being unable to say anything.[10] *Aporia* is a fundamental condition preparatory to discovery (as in the contemporary concept of falsification). A man must clearly recognize that he does not know at all (*to parapan*) just as Socrates says that he himself does not know at all what virtue is and that the Athenians do not know, and just as Meno has been shown not to know. This is operational ignorance, though to be sure it is not the absolute ignorance described by Whitehead as applying to whatever is unrelated to anything in the universe.[11] Rather it is an ignorance of where to seek a solution to a clearcut problem, shown in the inability to say anything at all. One's opinions, previously believed to be adequate, have been shown to be inadequate. One can name and describe the problem or object—"Meno," "virtue," "square double the area of a given square,"—but one is not acquainted with it. This is operational ignorance about the object in question, as the knower is now acquainted with his own limitations, namely, that his previous opinions were wrong in detail, his previous methods for thinking about the object are discredited, and no leads for a solution are in sight.

What has been created by the argument, however, is the recognition that a new principle or method is needed, that the answer cannot be got in the old rational way. The failure is not due to mere miscalculation[12] or simple logical inconsistency. Though the problem of doubling the square can be stated arithmetically in terms of a simple integer ratio, 1:2, the solution of side lengths cannot be reached by giving a simple integer ratio. The method of approximation from the original two through four to three-foot lengths cannot do the job.[13] The old rational (as rote) method has indicated that a rational (ratio of integers) number cannot be a solution to the problem, that is, that the relative standard of any arbitrarily chosen unit of length cannot be a measure of the length of the line sought, though the argument does not refer to incommensurable lines or irrational numbers. However, the reasoning does show the necessity for an extension beyond the familiar and beyond the integer ratios.

Part C: New Descriptive Extension. A new method is required. Socrates introduces it by pointing to a line in a diagram, the diagonal. This movement from using approximative techniques in identifying countable units to pointing at lines in a diagram (84A) does not indicate a less rigorous method but rather a more complex, "higher" level of mathematical analysis: from a line identified by its number of units to a line which divides the original area or square. The change clearly occurs at the descriptive level, as in the original attempt to identify by foot lengths, but the new description promises more success, being directly identified in terms of its function within the area in question. We move from arithmetic to geometry (or from linear geometry to plane geometry)—from routine rational methods to the first operation needed to grasp the geometrical relations. This is an operational casting of the problem itself and of knowing as discovering, so appropriate for a dialogue centering on the notion of the acquisition of goods.

Pointing at the diagonal is both a visual and a conceptual operation, for the line is identified *conceptually* as going from corner to corner of the square. Plato is thus not separating the empirical from the conceptual, but rather drawing the conceptual out of the visual, as Taylor notes.[14] This same point is fundamental in grasping the force of "our" (*hemin*) as Socrates redraws the figure in the sand and asks: "Is this not our four-foot square?" (84D). For after the redrawing, the figure now carries with it the properties previously established, both positive from part A and negative from part B. In this sense, it is less purely sensible than when originally drawn. Further, the figure is "ours" not because it is physically in front of us, but because despite its being a different sensible object from the original one, it is still the same four-equi-sided figure, each side of two-foot length. Socrates' striving for form within the realm of the sensible thus indicates the continuity of the inquiry as it returns to the basic problem of the first part and builds within the mind, necessarily prepared for grasping a novel concept as created by the second part.[15] Thus the move from part B to part C involves both continuity and discontinuity. Continuity derives from the intrinsic connection between preparing for a discovery and achieving it; discontinuity is implicit in the move from mechanically rational descriptions to a completely novel descriptive framework necessary for discovery.[16]

Socrates has noted that a given square *has (echon)* equal sides (82C), while in asking about the diagonals of squares of equal sides, he asks whether they *become (gignontai—85A)* equal. This linguistic nuance indicates clearly the difference between acknowledging the posited equality of the sides of the square and asserting the provability of the equality of corner-to-corner lines. More to the point in this difference, however, the altering of language from "having" to "becoming" is correlated with the initial use of a *cause*.[17]

Socrates constructs a framework in which the causal structure is elicited. After redrawing "our" square, Socrates draws two more squares round the same point, and asks whether they can "fill in this one in the corner?" (84D–E). For the boy to grasp that there is a space in which to draw a fourth square in the corner, when there is no visible corner as such, he must already have been led by sensible devices toward a notion of the total figure, so that it can serve as a framework.[18] Within this framework, however, the diagonal of the original square (4 square feet) serves as the productive cause of the double square (8 square feet). This line is internal to the original square but is seen to be the cause in the context of the total figure (16 square feet).

The diagonal is discovered as the generative cause dividing the original square into isosceles right triangles which then function as the constitutive causes of the double square. Socrates achieves this new view of size and shape by introducing the four-square framework. These isosceles right triangles are the units of area upon which the argument rests, as shown in the way the arithmetic is applied to the geometric problem. Socrates does *not* argue that since the diagonal divides the original square (4) into two equal parts, each part (a triangle) consists of two square feet and four such parts add up to eight square feet. This would have reduced the triangular area to the original square feet. Rather, he argues that the original square consists of two triangular areas, but the newly constructed square consists of four such areas. He then introduces some arithmetic: since "four is twice two," the area of the constructed square is twice that of the original square, therefore eight square feet. The answer in terms of square feet is only a special instance of a more general argument based on the isosceles right triangles as the unit of area. The causal analysis is thus a complex of 1) the framework (16-unit square), 2) the generative principle (the diagonal), and 3) the constitutive elements (the right triangles).

That this causal complex is the critical feature of the slave-boy episode receives clear emphasis when Socrates refers to it as evidence that remembering is knowing: "True opinions . . . are not worth much until you fasten them up with the causal reasoning (*aitias logismōi*). But this, my dear Meno, is remembering, as we agreed before. When they are fastened up, first they become knowledge. Once they are tied down, they become knowledge and then are stable. That is why knowledge is more honored than right opinion. What distinguishes knowledge from right opinion is the bond" (97E–98A—we have modified Rouse's translation). In identifying the diagonal as the generative cause of the double square, what has been determined adequately for the occasion (though not proved in an ultimate sense) is first that the length is not rational or subject to purely rational methods of determination (pt. B), and that as a line relating the original square to its double, it is an absolutely determinate relationally identifiable line. Its length in standard units (parts of a foot) is clearly unspecified and unspecifiable. It is an absolutely determinate new standard of length. Questions about the relation of this new one to the arbitrarily chosen standard of a foot are not raised in this argument (see sec. iv). These extended mathematical points are clearly implicit in Socrates' reflection upon the slave-boy's cognitive state of mind.

The slave-boy is said to have "had opinions stirred up in him as in a dream" (85C). These are, however, "true opinions" (86A) and can be stabilized. And Socrates says that the same questions asked in a variety of forms will improve the boy's understanding (85C–D). The movement from true opinion to knowledge, back to true opinion, and then forward again to knowledge marks this whole passage, emphasizing by this that knowing is the act of discovering, the coming-into-awareness of the causal reasonings.[19] No doubt the boy grasps the geometric causes only indistinctly at the end of the initial argument, whereas in the second part he is facile with the rote arithmetic. To regard well-grooved routines as above the level of indistinct causes is to make the error of the cave dwellers (*Republic* VII).

Though various terms for *knowing* and *knowledge* are used in the argument (*eidenai*—84A, 884B; *epistēsetai*, *epistēmē*—85D; *anamimnēskesthai*—84A, 85D; *analambanein*—85D) and the basic Socratic distinction between *epistēmē* and *alētheis doxai* underpins the total analysis, the basic point is that knowing is discovering and stabilizing in the mind causal connections between diverse objects—thus constituting a solid new entity. No proof or justification is required; it is embedded in the act of discovery itself.

In summary, the slave-boy episode illustrates discovery as a movement from one object, known by acquaintance (a square as a duly specified figure) through a descriptive extension to a related object (the double square) to a new conceptual framework in which one acquires the causal link constituting the new entity—now an object of acquaintance knowledge.

(iii)   *Socratic Assessment of the Episode*

With the demonstration a success, Socrates scrutinizes the result, mainly for its educative and practical value. Although the slave-boy is now said to be in a position to move ahead under further questioning, he is not said to be in the process of a dialectical ascent, in the way that in *Republic* VII the learning of plane geometry is, in large measure, for the sake of ascent to solid geometry and ultimately to dialectic. Rather the next stage envisaged for the boy is a more accurate grasp of the same finite geometrical connections he has just discovered. Nor is a different logic needed for this more stable grasp, for it will result from the boy's being asked the *same* questions in various forms (85C).

The hypothesis of recollection does support the doctrine of the immortality of the soul. But even this does not imply a hierarchy. Immortality is presented as a temporal line, appropriate to the dialogue's earlier grounding of recollection in the view that all nature is akin. The emphasis is on the question of how this view and its consequences lead to a commitment to inquire, though without positing any universal good. Supported now by the slave-boy's discovery, the position established enables Socrates to say that belief in inquiry makes man better and braver than disbelief in it, and that this belief is one for which he will fight in word and deed (*diischurisaimēn*, *diamachoimēn*—86 B–C). Thus the sequence which began with the myth as providing motives to inquire has moved through an inquiry to its consequences.

(iv)   *Some Implications of the Argument*

We should emphasize the clear-cut limitations of this illustration for the philosophy of mathematics as a basis in turn for reassessing its significance in the flow of Plato's argument.

The State of Mathematics. The argument exhibits mathematical knowledge which had been attained perhaps as much as one hundred years before Plato. It does not mention the problem of ordering incommensurable lines—a problem which developed from questions, also raised much earlier, about the relation of the side and diagonal of a square.[20] The *Meno* therefore is not imparting the latest word about geometrical knowledge. Nor is it criticizing the science for its lack of discoveries—this would be presumptuous indeed. There is no evidence that Plato ever judged "badness" or "goodness" of a science by its condition at a given moment in history, even when he recognized the undeveloped state of solid geometry (*Republic* VII).

The Use of Images in Mathematics. B. L. Van der Waerden has wisely raised the issue of the Greek use of images in geometry in a comprehensive historical context. He asks: "Why did the Greeks not simply adopt Babylonian algebra as it was, why did they put it in geometric form? Was it their delight in the tangible and visible, which turned them away from number, to occupy themselves with figures instead?"[21] Though admitting the powerful images in Greek literature, he argues that for the Pythagoreans numbers were "the rock bottom of the entire universe." Turning to geometry as a visual science was contrary to their conception of the substantive nature of number. Therefore the urge to geometrize algebra originated in the discovery of the incommensurability of the diagonal with the side of a square. "It is therefore logical necessity, not the mere delight in the visible, which compelled the Pythagoreans to transmute their algebra into geometric form."[22] In fact, no amount of sense imagery could ever bring a person to the conception of incommensurable magnitudes. Van der Waerden's argument shows clearly that the Pythagoreans before the time of Plato knew that they were reasoning about ideals and their relationships, not about sensible objects per se. The later solution to the ordering of incommensurables (by Theaetetus and Eudoxus) would then have been in no way needed to establish the fact that geometry was not grounded essentially or solely in images.

Euclid's illustrations (lines instead of dots, even in books of arithmetic) are presumably more general representations appropriate to the greater generality of the arguments and are not designed to replace the proof structure.

Arpad Szabo has argued for the solidification of Greek deductive thought (as found primarily in Euclidean proofs) from a period when demonstration was essentially a simple showing or visualizing to a later one when the showing turned primarily upon the deductive structure.[23] The development of indirect proofs by the Eleatics (Parmenides and Zeno) and their application to mathematical subject matter occurred about the beginning of the fifth century B.C. Certainly by the end of the fifth century, according to the well-established historical knowledge of Greek mathematics,[24] the deductive structure of large portions of Euclidean mathematics had been established.

The Use of Images in Plato. The occurrence of an image in a Platonic argument is not itself indicative of a "lower" level of analysis. The question is, rather, how the image functions. If it is used to raise queries about quantity, measurement, causal relations, and so forth, an image moves one toward dialectic, discovery, and knowledge; if it merely occasions the naming of an entity sensed or imagined, an image leads nowhere and generates opinions (*Republic* 523C–524D).[25]

Knowledge in the Phaedo *as Recollection.* The doctrines of recollection in the *Phaedo* and in the *Meno* are sometimes interpreted as being the same.[26] Yet the *Phaedo* emphasizes the separation of soul and body, which are respectively more akin to ideal forms and sensible copies, while the *Meno* stresses the drawing of forms from sensible images, as we have argued above. The problems of the two dialogues are quite different, the latter centering on acquisition of goods, the former on the immortality of the soul. Differing accounts of a given theory are given in different dialogues. This hints at the complexity of the concept in question, as revealed in the several structures of thought.

Philosophy of Mathematics in the Meno. As we indicated earlier, knowledge in the *Meno* is conceived as involving acquaintance with the object known. So the mathematics of the *Meno* emphasizes coming-to-know or discovery in direct contrast with the formal hierarchy of mathematical (physical and social) sciences of the *Republic* VII. Inquiry, discovery, or the eliciting of proof from an instance by finding the appropriate causal middle connecting the beginning with the conclusion, constitutes knowledge which needs no further justification. This general point contrasts with the later proof (in the section on argument by hypothesis, 86D–89C) that virtue is teachable. The form of that proof is strictly deductive. It depends upon identifying virtue with knowledge as the ever-present element in all that is useful for man. The link, however, between knowledge and usefulness is not established by the kind of internal link between figures which operates in the slave-boy episode, but only by repeated experiences of an association of knowledge with the useful.

The "externally" related concepts, presented in a deductive schema which produces a conclusion ultimately superseded, contrast with concepts internally related in a context of discovery of a connecting "middle." The latter, in turn, yields an argument exerting a momentum toward a conclusion which, when found, holds fast. This suggests that the conception of mathematics in the *Meno* is more closely akin to the twentieth-century constructive-intuitive philosophy of mathematics than to formalist or logicist conceptions.

The intuitionists' argument that the proof is contained in the properly constructed and intuited relationships and that no extraneous justification is needed is quite like the identity in the *Meno* of the solution achieved with its very discovery. This philosophy of mathematics rests ultimately on the role of the human mind in the process of discovery, although we make no claim that Plato anticipated any of the versions of twentieth-century philosophy of mathematics.

(v)   *The Human Mind*

It is generally accepted that Plato used as interlocutors in his dialogues men whom history testifies had characters and minds fitting well the parts they played in the dialogues. Certainly Protagoras, Euthyphro, and Meno could not have appropriately replaced each other in the dialogues now identified by their names. It seems reasonable, therefore, that Plato in constructing the slave-boy episode, has chosen as interlocutor just the type of person he feels could illustrate his main points.

a) He needs someone as completely removed from the Greek cultural scene as possible, yet able to communicate in the Greek language. Most educated Greeks knew the geometrical truth he wanted to elicit from the slave-boy. Plato cannot exhibit the learning process (recollection) in any simple way if he uses such sophisticates. Further, the spontaneous response of such an uneducated person will produce the expected mechanically rational answers leading to *aporia,* which necessitates the reorientation by means of which the discovery is made.

b) A truth such as this, immediately available to an ordinary person at the lowest rung of the social scale, attests to the fact that the knowledge acquired is universally available to all men. It is public and objective knowledge which is attainable. However tenuous a hold on this truth the slave-boy has by virtue of what he has undergone so rapidly, he is at least turned now in the right direction.

The point is not simply that all men are able to grasp such truths, but that *to have a mind at all is to undergo such learning experiences.* The later argument bears this out negatively when it shows that virtue is not teachable because it is not taught, for the assumption is that if the subject were teachable, the minds capable of learning it are available.

The outstanding instance to support this conception of the human mind is the slave-boy with his capacity to learn. Socrates first asks

Meno to call whichever one of his attendants Meno pleases, and after Meno has done this Socrates establishes that he is Greek and speaks Greek (82B). Yet the conclusion is applied to human nature in general (86B). This combination of Greek setting (Athens-Larisa) and the universal nature of the problem provides another instance of the combination of idealistic structure with an operational point of focus.[27]

c) The fact that learning constitutes the very mind of man suggests that knowledge is not a matter of mere agreement, common or repetitious experiences, or definition, but rather arises from the very logic of the relation between concepts—the internal causal structure revealed at least partially in a single exposure to the relationship. No "forceful impression" could convey the truth of the relation. Certainly the truth is not evident in an uninterpreted diagram. Only one who has followed the argument understands the nature of the problem and its solution. In this sense, the object of knowledge merges with the mind of the knower.

This is in direct contrast with the Cartesian searches for clear and distinct ideas, and with Humean impressions or any other "perspectival grounds" for live knowledge in an analysis of true beliefs. And it provides a different basis for our theory of mind; for example, for our knowledge of other minds, self-knowledge, and self-identity.

d) Even the later (97A–B) treatment of experiential knowing which is more nearly akin to the type of knowledge based on impressions, and so forth, is in the *Meno* grounded in this more fundamental type of conceptual knowledge. Plato does not use this latter type to transcend the experiential level, but uses it to illuminate the knowledge of particulars in our experience. A clue to this is found in the analogy of the path connecting Larisa to Athens with the diagonal connecting the two squares, though the kind of connection is clearly different (see chap. 7).

e) The human mind is thus not some simple input-output entity as B. F. Skinner supposes. It goes beyond the input, providing within itself something vital, giving significance to the input. The emphasis is not on some generalized source of forms as it is in the *Phaedo*. Nor is there some underlying generalized formal structure in the mind to which all knowledge must conform, whether it be of a sort cherished by Kant or Chomsky. All that is revealed is the particular causal link within a properly framed problem, hitherto descriptively identified. The possible extent of the capacity of the mind to discover new relations is completely open and indeterminate.

f) In chapters 1 and 2 we rejected the conventional being-becoming distinction between an intelligible and sensible world as yielding a rigid opposition between what virtue is and how it is acquired. We suggested a more flexible conception of the *ti-poion* distinction, applicable at every level of analysis and thought in Plato's definitional dialectic. The argument that the *Meno* expresses mere becoming or passage, misses the subtlety; there is nothing "unplatonic" in asking for the being of change, motion, generation, or acquisition. For example, Galileo's law of falling bodies expresses the form or being of accelerated motion for bodies near the earth's surface. The slave-boy episode is not a statement of the form of knowledge, if there could be any such statement for Plato. By concentrating instead upon a given instance of inquiry and the acquisition of knowledge, the argument exhibits the way inquiry is conducted and knowledge acquired. The generation in the inquirer of the answer to the original problem constitutes the solution to the problem of learning. The structure of this inquiry is thus an example of the very form of this generation of knowledge, that is, of recollection. Forms emerge in the process both in the mathematical truth self-disclosed by the slave-boy and in the philosophical truth self-disclosed by Socrates and the slave-boy together as they exhibit the being of generation in the very act of generating or acquiring. This intimate connection of being and generation (or acquisition) in the slave-boy episode underlies the later solutions to the *poion* problem of the acquisition of virtue at Meno's level, though the process of acquisition in the two cases is not identical.

In summary, though we have here separated the mathematical implications (sec. iv) from the implications for a philosophy of mind (sec. v), the slave-boy episode itself makes no such separation. Discovery is not merely mathematical but also physical and psychological, involving perceptual and intuitive details. It is epistemological and metaphysical as well. As we have indicated, the justification or proof is contained within the discovery itself in contrast with the "deductive" mode of the hypothetical argument.

Thus Plato has shown how discoveries may be made by those who have mapped out a problem, eliminated the blind alleys in the search for an answer, and sought both within themselves and within the nature of the problem for the answer unique to the problem so exposed.

Part Two: The *Poion* Methods and Solution

4 Can Virtue Be Acquired by Being Taught?

Following the slave-boy episode, the dialogue returns to the *poion* question (86C–D). This poses a difficulty for readers who treat the first two parts of the dialogue as mainly providing definitive answers to primary questions. But Meno's original query, "How is virtue acquired?" determines the basic subject matter of the dialogue, and the early searches for what virtue is and for how knowledge is acquired are preparatory to providing an answer to the original one. The argument in the *Meno* does not move on virtue from an unsuccessful attempt to answer a fundamental question to a second-best treatment of it, as say, the *Phaedo*'s argument moves on the cause of change (from Anaxagoras' final cause to a conception of forms—99D) or the *Republic*'s on the idea of the good (506E). Rather, Meno's original question is a secondary one—one which cannot be answered by a direct approach at all. It requires that a structure be built in which an answer can be formulated. In this sense the first two parts of the dialogue have prepared negatively for this effort by their failures respectively to achieve a definition and to persuade Meno to seek one, and we shall see that positively some features of these initial sections guide the change, though only within sharp limitations.

A sudden reversal in the interlocutors' roles signals the change. Up to this point Socrates has been in control, keeping attention on the *ti* question of what virtue is, by successively overcoming Meno's tendency to bypass or to resist it. This control becomes tightest when Socrates gives the slave-boy's discovery as the ground for renewing the definitional search, and Meno momentarily agrees. But then the peripety occurs (86C), as we have seen in chap. 1.

Up to this reversal Socrates' position had been that he could not tell how virtue is acquired without knowing what it is. The shift to the problem of acquisition has been prepared for in the earlier definitional section, since the final definition of virtue was in terms of acquiring goods, and even the last model definition (by Socrates) was similarly in terms of how we come to possess sense impressions. But the new element is a fundamental one for as a *poion* question it must determine how man comes to have virtue independently of considerations of what it is.

Critics have generally overlooked the immediate significance of this new formulation of the problem, that is, that the inquiry must get its *starting* point not from any property of virtue, but from what can be posited about the way man acquires anything whatever. Indeed Socrates says he begins without knowing either what virtue is or what it is like (*hopoion ti*—87B). He must begin with a mode of acquisition, and the one he chooses is that of learning from teaching, and knowledge enters as the only thing taught. Just as this doctrine of acquisition is chosen apart from any property of virtue, so also knowledge enters simply as being teachable. Thus in his choice of teaching as the mode of acquisition upon which to center, his inquiry has narrowed to one of the disjunctive alternatives which Meno proposed (teaching, nature, practice, or some other way—70A). Such emphasis on the primary cognitive notion of acquisition is in keeping with the slave-boy demonstration that knowledge is possible for man. Socrates refers back to that episode in now being willing to reduce remembering to the process of learning through being taught (87B).

Another reversal has occurred here. The slave-boy's achievement can now be viewed as a kind of learning through teaching, since Socrates gave symbolic guidance to the boy, as some interpreters maintain.[1] And with teaching thus treated generically as symbolic guidance, it can be given the disjunctive character Meno proposed for it, that is, as exclusive of or at least prior to other modes of acquisition. For example, acquiring by nature, would have to mean acquiring without outside symbolic stimulus of any kind; otherwise teaching is occurring. (Socrates will say later that if virtue is wisdom it does not come by nature—89A.) The net effect is to maintain in the *poion* section the concentration of the dialogue on the question whether virtue is knowledge (though leaving open thereby the question whether a definition is not being smuggled in).

The model for the inquiry is hypothetical geometrical reasoning. The use of the geometrical model (87A) is in keeping with the earlier uses of the definition of figure and of the double square problems as models.[2] This also retains the idealist or cognitive element. If, however, the model is to be geometrical, why not use the double-square, that is, why not analogize virtue and teachability respectively to the square and its double? Plato's not using the double-square analogy makes the adaptation to the *poion* problem more evident. Success in using this analogy would have depended upon establishing an internal link between virtue and teachability, since the square and its double constitute a determinate subject matter inherently containing that link. The problem now, though, is that of relating virtue to teachability *without* the internal knowledge of virtue (or, indeed, of teachability, as we shall see) necessary to constitute such a subject matter. The argument by hypothesis is intended to resolve this problem.

(i)   *Two Textual Problems*

An adequate interpretation of the ensuing argument by hypothesis has proved difficult for two reasons: a) Some have incorrectly believed that this particular argument by hypothesis should be the same as other Platonic treatments of arguments by hypothesis, such as are found in the *Phaedo*, and b) some keen interpreters have devised ingenious accounts of the passage, misled as they have been by Plato's elliptical language—accounts which really miss the force of the argument in the progress of the dialogue. As for the first, we shall indicate shortly the special sense of argument by hypothesis in the *Meno* in contrast to other possible uses by Plato. As for the second, we shall simply offer here our conclusions about the proper reading of two vexing passages, having elsewhere presented our detailed examinations of fine points raised by other interpreters.[3]

1) As noted above, Socrates' problem is that of establishing a relation between virtue and teachability without knowledge of the nature of either. For this he suggests that they use the mathematician's hypothetical method which he illustrates by a geometrical model. The geometrical hypothesis (87A3–5) is: "If the space is such that when you apply it to the given line of the circle, it is deficient by a space of the same size as that which has been applied, one thing appears to

follow, and if this is impossible, another."[4] We read "the given line of the circle" as being the side of an equilateral triangle which would be inscribed in the circle, this being also the base line of the area as inscribed in the circle. The area is applied to this line in accord with Euclid's *Elements*, Book II, Proposition 14 and Book VI, Proposition 11. If this same area, now in the shape of a rectangle, can be drawn again "above" its original application and remain within the diameter of the circle which bisects the side of the original equilateral triangle, then the area is inscribable, and if not, not. Our interpretation provides a genuine *diorismos*, which Plato's problem requires. The knowledge for understanding this was available to educated Greeks of Plato's day and is available to any ninth-grade student of geometry.

2) The second passage which has occasioned so much ingenious interpretation is the concluding sentence of the argument by hypothesis, a sentence now generally read: "And plainly, Socrates, on our hypothesis that virtue is knowledge, it must be taught" (89C).[5] This reading has led many present-day interpreters to conclude that Plato is stating that one of the primary hypotheses is, "Virtue is knowledge." We have examined much of the voluminous literature on this point but still believe this is a misreading. We read the passage as: "And it is plain, Socrates, on our hypothesis, since virtue is knowledge, that it is teachable." In this reading, the word *hypothesis* is not in apposition with anything, but is referring to the basic hypothesis of the argument-by-hypothesis: "Knowledge alone is teachable." From this basic supposition the major premise of a hypothetical syllogism is derivable: "If virtue is knowledge, clearly it could be taught" (see derivation below). Meno's summary statement at 89C thus refers to and uses, but does not repeat, the original hypothesis; but his point is rather that since the antecedent of that major premise has been proved (this antecedent is also the minor premise of the syllogism—"virtue is knowledge"), then the conclusion of the syllogism—"virtue is teachable"—is justified in a simple *modus ponens* inference (see sec. ii, d, below). This reading fits the facts and overcomes the difficulties envisaged by various interpreters.

(ii)   *Formal Structure of the Argument*

Plainly, no adequate account of the argument by hypothesis is possible if one is misled by taking the admittedly difficult Greek as suggesting that a step in the argument is that "Virtue is knowledge" is a hypothesis rather than a proposition—both proved and used as a premise for a further proof. Having rid ourselves of this notion, we can now easily describe the formal structure of the argument as it emerges in four clearly distinguishable steps.

a) In the first step, Plato illustrates the formal structure of a hypothetical argument with the geometrical example and then uses it as a guide in searching for an appropriate hypothesis. Socrates thus looks for a universal equivalence-statement to serve the same purpose for his modeled argument which the geometrical equivalence-statement has served in its turn, that is, as a criterion as to whether or not a given property is ascribable to a given object. He then supposes that "virtue is a quality among the things which are about the soul;" that is, virtue is "like or unlike knowledge" (87B—Rouse, trans.).

b) From this *ad hoc* supposition of an equivalence property, Socrates draws his universal equivalence-statement, which presumably has universal acceptance or at least finds favor with Meno: "Knowledge alone is teachable" (87C). This is his first and major hypothesis. The second is presented as a practical tautology—also universally acceptable. It is "Virtue is a good thing" (87D).

c) From these hypotheses, Socrates derives two further statements that now serve as the premises of a hypothetical syllogism. From "Knowledge alone is teachable," he gets the major premise of the hypothetical syllogism by what we, today, would call a formally valid two-step procedure. Since the hypothesis is an equivalence-statement, it is equivalent to the conjunction of a universal material implication and its converse, that is, "whatever is knowledge is teachable and whatever is teachable is knowledge." From this, either of the two implications is validly derivable and Socrates uses only the first of them, "whatever is knowledge is teachable." The second step is simply the existential instantiation of this universal statement, using virtue as the object of instantiation. (See below our arguments for treating the concept, virtue, as an object.) This yields "if virtue is knowledge, then it is teachable" (87C) which is the major premise of the hypothetical syllogism. (There it reads: "Then if virtue is knowledge, clearly it could be taught.")

The derivation of the minor premise of the syllogism from the second hypothesis "Virtue is a good thing" requires an induction which we shall examine below. This derivation constitutes the substance of what is called the argument by hypothesis. "Virtue is knowledge" is thus proved, is not a hypothesis, and does in turn function as the minor premise of the hypothetical syllogism which is the formal core of the argument.

d) The conclusion of the hypothetical syllogism is "Virtue is teachable." It follows from the joint assertion of the two premises noted above by a simple *modus ponendo ponens* rule of inference.[6] There is nothing mysterious about this argument by hypothesis from the formal point of view. In fact, once the linguistic elements are clarified, the formal structure is obvious—it is as direct and formally impeccable as any simple deduction in an elementary logic class.

The formal universal equivalence-relationship which the major hypothesis expresses, taken with the particular existence statement that an object has one of the stated properties, thus correctly yields the conclusion that the object has the second equivalent property. This structure of the argument is clear in both the geometrical model and the moral argument. The parts of these arguments are quite analogous: the area and circle to virtue; the applicability or non-applicability of the area to the "given line" to knowledge or not knowledge; and the inscribability or non-inscribability to teachable or non-teachable. The arguments neither of the model nor of what is modeled are grounded in the nature of things. The method is appropriate to the *poion* problem, for it organizes and systematizes our opinions in "proof" form. This argument by hypothesis contrasts sharply with arguing dialectically from hypotheses to first principles as Plato describes argument at the fourth level of the divided line. Neither is it a simple deduction of subsidiary concepts as is presumably the argument from the third level of the divided line in *Republic* VII. Rather, it is an instantiation of a universal proposition.

Similarly, the method is not that of determining the nature of a thing by defining a concept or discovering a causal linkage; but, rather, that of using a noncausal middle for attaching or detaching a universal property to or from an object. The method provides a sharp yes/no discrimination, though based on a free-floating principle, as appropriate for a *poion* problem. Relationships are established but no definitions are given; for example, "virtue is knowledge" is not a definition of a nature. This method yields a formally valid argument, regardless of content—a most unusual separation for Plato. The basic distinction between knowledge and opinion, which is fundamental in the opening sections of the dialogue (see chaps. 2–3) is operative here, and is further developed in the final section of the dialogue (see chap. 7).

(iii)   *Knowledge Alone is Teachable*

One might ask, on formal grounds: Why did Plato present as hypotheses statements of greater content than were needed as premises for his hypothetical syllogism? The answer to this must be seen in the contrast of the principle of this argument with those of the definition and slave-boy sections. Rather than seeking the essence of virtue or a causal middle between extremes, the new *poion* section appeals to consequences. This appeal governs the remainder of the dialogue. In the present argument by hypothesis, it appears in two ways: 1) teaching is the consequence being attached to virtue and determines the significance of the concept, knowledge, and 2) knowledge is attached to virtue in establishing the minor premise of the hypothetical syllogism (see sec. iv below). In this section, we concentrate upon the major hypothesis in which knowledge and teaching are equated.

Perhaps, since Socrates here teaches Meno by an argument from hypothesis, we will see what "teaching" now means. The exclusively cognitive character of learning by teaching is indicated in its being knowledge "alone" and in its being distinct from a natural development, and at least logically separable from practical training. Such teaching is clearly distinct from that which all citizens give the young in *Protagoras* and from the imitations of models and habituation in *Republic* III. Similarly, since being taught is also called "recollection" in an explicit echo from the slave-boy proof (87B), proof must be involved, thereby differentiating this teaching sharply from the indoctrination of impressionable souls in *Republic* II. On the other hand, since learning as recollection is reduced to the assimilation of externally transmitted knowledge, if falls far short of the conversion of the soul accomplished by the dialectical teaching in *Republic* VII. This teaching thus seems to lie somewhere between the practical teaching of the *Protagoras* and the internal process of understanding which the slave-boy has just experienced.

Such a description of teaching closely fits Socrates' hypothetical argument; that is, the application of *ad hoc* hypotheses to given cases to yield determinate *yes* or *no* answers. It is a deductive argument exhibited symbolically and showing a practical conclusion; for example, teaching prudence in eating as in Aristotle's practical syllogism from the *Nichomachean Ethics* (1141b18–21); one can conclude "This chicken is easily digestible" from "All light meat is easily digestible" and "This chicken is light meat."

The argument by which Socrates teaches Meno that virtue is teachable has the same logical form, and "knowledge alone is teachable" must be interpreted by its function in this context. The fact that teaching and knowledge are convertible terms provides the *ad hoc* hypothesis on which to base the deduction. What is signified by the proposition is important and sharp, but limited—namely, that one knows about a thing when one can produce the relevant argument about it, and one teaches about it when one conveys this knowledge in this syllogistic formal way to another person. No other kind of knowledge is envisaged, and no other kind of communication is allowed in setting up this hypothetical proposition.

The formal structure of the argument in modern logical terms involves the instantiation of the major premise and the application of the *modus ponens* rule of inference. The formal necessity of this argument structure is obvious, and this type of hypothetical reasoning is quite the same as the twentieth-century covering-law argument which has served for many thinkers as the paradigm of scientific proof—an argument in which a universal hypothesis or law is applied to an existential instance. The derived conclusion in Plato's case accordingly has a different status from the conclusion of the geometrical model, since moral proof may serve as a prediction of an outcome testable by observation, which, in turn, may confirm (verify?) or disconfirm (falsify) the original premises. Plato is of course sensitive to the difference, and the problem of the existential testing of the outcome or conclusion of Plato's argument is developed in the Anytos episode (chaps. 5 and 6). In the formal structure and in this emphasis on existential testing of the consequences, the modern covering-law argument and Plato's argument by hypothesis are identical, though the philosophies built upon this common structure are of course quite different.

For Plato, if virtue is knowledge and is teachable, then presumably it consists of known universal premises or rules properly applied to particular instances of action. The whole problem of the argument by hypothesis thus centers upon proving that "Virtue is indeed knowledge."

(iv)   Inductive "Proof" of "Virtue is Knowledge"

In chapter 2, we stated that "being acquainted with virtue" was analogized to "being acquainted with Meno" as a basis for knowing anything about an object. Further, we showed that the geometrical illustration of the argument by hypothesis exemplified the application of a universal hypothesis to a particular case. This suggests now that "virtue" refers to some particular object. Socrates' introduction of the second hypothesis reinforces this determination. He asks; "Don't we say that virtue is a good thing?" And the second hypothesis drawn from this is, "virtue is good," or the thing, virtue, has the property, good.

Interpretation must show why Plato gives as a second hypothesis more than is needed to complete the hypothetical syllogism ("Virtue is knowledge"), and derives this premise by a lengthy argument from "Virtue is good." This derivation in fact, constitutes the bulk of this argument.

The form of the argument is simple. Plato equates "good with "useful" (*ōphelimos*—87E), thus deriving "Virtue is useful." From this, by an inclusive induction, he establishes "Whatever is useful is [or involves] knowledge." This latter proposition taken with the former yields, "Virtue is knowledge," which, with the major premise, in turn, yields "Virtue is teachable." The selection of the second hypothesis, "Virtue is good," thus provides for the formal structure in which identities are established, but the definition of virtue is neither known nor sought. The inquiry thus turns on empirically testable consequences.

The induction begins with the observable state, health, and moves through other observable states, namely, strength, beauty, wealth, to show that these are useful when (through guidance) they are rightly used. As for states of the soul, those which are not knowledge (*episteme*) are useful when used with mind (*nous*). Temperance (*sophrosyne*) and intelligence (cleverness—*eumathia*) without mind are harmful. Finally, all behavior and endurances or dispositions in the soul, when guided by wisdom (*phronesis*), "end in happiness (*eudaimonia*)" (88C). The argument thus moves from what is physically observable, where guiding conditions are noted by outcomes achieved (useful vs. harmful), through states of the soul, to activities of the soul led by wisdom as the principle of attaining the goal of life, happiness. Health, for example, is not an internal principle or structure of the body analogized to a similar structure in the soul; it is rather an observable bodily state (i.e., by a physician) whose effects can be useful or harmful. From such an observable state, the argument points to a comparable state of an *un*observable entity, the soul, but not in order to analogize its internal well-being with that of the body. Rather, it argues that the goodness of the soul depends upon the element in its dispositional structure which produces, over the long run, a stable, happy outcome.

In summary, all external things are made useful by the soul, and things of the soul in order to be good must depend on wisdom. Since the good is the same as the useful, the useful is wisdom; and finally, since virtue is useful, virtue is either wholly or partly wisdom. The induction thus extracts the cognitive element and establishes the universal tie between the object which is virtue, and knowledge. The presence or absence of the "intervening variable" (knowledge) is shown by the empirical utilitarian consequences (useful or harmful).

The force of such empirical-inductive arguments depends not merely upon the rigor of the empirical techniques employed or of the inductive procedures of generalization from the data, but more upon the classification of kinds of actions and their outcomes. The classification of outcomes in terms of the utilitarian principle (useful or harmful) reduces the theoretical structure to that of a simple yes or no.

This inductively established universal empirical tie is not a rigorous conceptual one, and in no case are the consequences held to be those peculiar to virtue. In other places Plato does seek ties between virtues and consequences (e.g., *Republic*, IV and IX, where the just man is shown to enjoy advantages over the unjust, tyrannical man). The tie here, however, is explicitly existential. Further, the argument does not characterize the knowledge associated with virtue in any way except to indicate its consequences. Knowledge is held in this empirical argument to be existentially equivalent to (or convertible with) the practical term, *useful*. The argument is based wholly on invariably observed associations of useful with knowledge and of harmful with ignorance.

If a person were to object that sometimes our knowledge leads us to make judgments that are not useful, he would be contradicting the terms of the argument; for if the consequences are not useful, then the judgment was folly, lacking in sense. There is no distinction between knowledge well-used and knowledge ill-used; ill-use marks the absence of knowledge altogether. Thus, knowledge and its absence exhaust the possibilities in a context in which the existential consequences are the useful and the harmful, the not-useful being included in the harmful. The useful is thus the existential criterion of the knowledge on which it is said to depend.

This emphasis on consequences extends through the whole third part of the *Meno*. Thus the argument that virtue does not come about "by nature" is based on the fact that if it did so arise, no external guide would have been needed and outward signs of the power within would have been evident. Further, the shift to consequences accounts for the locus of the virtues sought in the subsequent argument with Anytos (chaps. 5 and 6). There the good or virtuous men are political figures, and the prime virtue is usefulness to the state—usefulness, not as Socrates is useful, but as men of action are. This, as ascribable to historical figures such as Pericles, puts the emphasis on virtue as possessed, thus allowing for its empirical identification without a definition of it. When to this is added the politico-actional emphasis required by the shift to consequences, we have full warrant for the return, in the Anytos episode, to the historical setting provided by the city-states to which the participants belong. Finally, the notion of consequences governs the final argument of the dialogue where the notion of the useful is the determining principle (see chap. 7). This use of consequences shows what we mean when we say that these arguments are operationally determined. The usual Platonic questions about the useful are passed over in this consequential argument— questions such as "Useful for what?" "Useful under what conditions?" "Useful as just or good?" or the converse of this last. Here the useful is identified with the good, emphasizing the existential character and values of the argument. A dialectic of the good in itself is bypassed in this dialogue.

On the other hand, there is no problem of going from "is" to "ought" simply because the value is stated as existentially given. What this means for our purposes—and what the derivation of "Virtue is knowledge" from "Virtue is useful" shows directly—is that "knowledge" is not separable from the values or ends achieved by its use. Rather, the end, that is, the useful, is directly bound up with the knowledge.

This contrasts with the *Protagoras* where the end, the maximizing of pleasure and minimizing of pain, is held quite separate from the knowledge employed to achieve the end—the calculation of pleasures and pains in which the primary problem is not to underestimate distantly future pleasures and pains in making the calculation. (It also contrasts with Russell and others who separate sharply the scientifically formulable from the realm of value—knowledge being merely useful as a nonvaluative technical device in achieving objects of desire or aversion.) In the *Meno* the good is identical with the useful and the useful entails and is entailed by knowledge, not in the sense of being a mere technical tool toward an independently constituted value, but rather as that without which there is no value at all. The idealist dimension is thus intrinsically bound up with the operationist consequence, the useful.

Knowledge is thus an originative cause or source of value as the argument establishing the minor premise of the hypothetical argument develops. The implication of this point for value-free social science or for a purely theoretical structure or calculation of ideas independent of ends is clear. Some modern conceptions of science as a purely theoretical discipline appear to be amoral and non-humanist. Value-free research is based upon a logistical structure of knowledge in direct contrast to this action-oriented, operational sense of knowledge. Similarly, the sharp distinction of the philosophy of social science from social philosophy as concerned respectively with testability and tenability distorts both fields.[7]

Finally, this interpenetration (or equivalence) of knowledge and value carries over into Plato's summary of the proof that virtue is knowledge and therefore teachable. But Plato puts the word *epistēmē* instead of the word *phronēsis* in Meno's mouth (89C), though the latter word was used throughout the inductive argument establishing equivalence. An "identity" between *phronēsis* and *epistēmē* is thus achieved in this concluding summary argument that virtue is not given by nature and that it is acquired by education or learning (*mathēsis*). But the main point here is that the *phronēsis* which is necessary as a guide for men's actions to useful ends is identified with the *epistēmē* which is particularly applicable to hypothetically structured knowledge appropriate for didactic teaching and learning. In this context, the covering-law argument is completed by drawing the conclusion that virtue is teachable or taught. The conclusion is thus a prediction, and the existence or nonexistence of this predicted consequential state of affairs tends to confirm or disconfirm either or both premises.

(v)   *The Significance of the Argument*

We turn finally to the significance of this argument in the development of the *Meno*. That the conclusion as drawn is immediately questioned by Socrates and ultimately disproved raises the question why Plato retained an argument that he knew was faulty. Clearly, this argument does not have a cumulative dialectical structure such as the one which we discerned in the search for a definition of virtue (chap. 2). Nor is it the case of Plato slipping in his "true belief" in spite of Meno's not being up to it. Rather, it is a literally structured argument, the conclusion of which is shown to be literally and existentially false.

The turn from a search for what virtue is to a determination about its transmissibility entailed a shift in the meaning of the term *knowledge* from 1) a causally structured knowing or discovery to 2) an *ad hoc* hypothetical didactic determination and the subsequent assimilation of this didactic notion of knowledge to 3) knowledge as the guide to action, without which actions and dispositions of the soul are not useful but harmful.

Of course, the immediate purpose of setting the standard in the hypothetical didactic form is to point to the need for testing and altering it. Plato thus opens up a crucial question: Is didactic knowledge of the hypothetical kind appropriate for guiding our actions? Is this technical knowledge the source of the useful or good in action? These are significant questions still pointedly relevant. We may remember that President Kennedy learned to distrust "expert" knowledge in decision-making, for example, in the Bay of Pigs crisis. Or, to put the question conversely, is the kind of cognition by which we decide and act, and by which we build up dispositions to make such choices, really capturable through this geometrical way of reasoning about a particular case? Perhaps the application of geometrical reasoning to geometrical subject matter is quite simple as compared with its use in practical decision-making. This latter use introduces elements which may place in doubt the applicability of any given hypothesis to a given case.

In concentrating, however, upon cognition as a guide for action, Plato both sets the existential base of the problem in virtue-as-possessed and retains the idealistic orientation derived from the definitional and slave-boy sections. Further doubt is thrown on the argument when the succeeding Anytos episode shows that virtue is not taught. But the force of the hypothetical argument, even with its errors, is too strong to be dismissed, for it has carried forward the cognitive orientation of the sections on definition and recollection. Its knowledge is clearly not theirs. Although the guide to action is not knowledge in this strong sense, it can still be some form of cognition.

This presumption will set the final and principal problem of the dialogue: the relation of theory to action (chap. 7). The hypothetical argument at the same time, sets the outer limit of the cognitive as applicable to action—thus providing one of the boundaries to the problem.

Most important to the ambiguous use of "knowledge," Plato is setting up the first step in his movement from universal conceptual knowledge (slave-boy episode), through hypothetical universal cognitions, ultimately to cognitions of other kinds. What is notable here is that the content of the premises of any formally valid argument is central in determining whether or not what is being conveyed is indeed knowledge and not a less reliable form of cognition. The thought expressed by the major hypothesis of the primary argument "Knowledge alone is teachable" does not itself constitute knowledge even though the subject of the proposition is knowledge. As hypothesized, no causal connection is established between the concepts, knowledge and teachable, and the connection between the terms in the universal equivalence-proposition is not firmly established in the very minds of the men constructing the argument. Neither is the thought expressed by the major premise of the geometrical illustration (as hypothesized) knowledge, though the premise is sufficient to yield warranted opinion about the conclusion being sought. For example, the premise is based upon a connection not causally established, that the equilateral triangle is the triangle of maximum area inscribable within a circle. The movement, however, from such organized cognitions is a step toward our understanding of knowledge of particular facts—such particular facts being primarily concerned with human action or experience in its most immediate sense (chap. 7). Yet this step is not sufficient. One more is required—a step reflected in a social consensus on the value of accumulated human experience. This is found in the Anytos episode (chaps. 5–6).

In conclusion, then, the transmissibility of virtue may depend upon its being didactic knowledge and its existence and function as a useful guide in action may imply that it does have a cognitive dimension. Yet if it is not transmissible there may be an ineradicable difference between didactic knowledge and this cognitive function. The existential test of teaching may well reveal the possibilities of the ambiguity in the terms used in the hypothetical argument; but for just this reason the subsequent proof that virtue is not teachable does not undo Socrates' achievement in establishing a cognitive basis for the utility of virtue. This indicates both the limitations of his argument and its adaptation to the contours of fact. The test occurs in what is known as the Anytos episode of the *Meno*, so we shall examine this in the next two chapters.

5 The Anytos Episode A:
Structure of the Argument

To make an empirical test of whether virtue is teachable, the Anytos episode[1] looks at educational practices in Athens and Thessaly. Finding no teachers of virtue, Socrates concludes that it is not teachable. This argument fares well within the dialogue itself but not in critical literature. Robert Hoerber cites it to illustrate the "loose reasoning" in the latter part of the dialogue: "The absence of instructors and students in any subject, for example, does not mean necessarily that the particular subject is not teachable."[2] It is variously said to be "dubious" as a demonstration,[3] in "the shadow of Meno's *amathia*,"[4] "not serious."[5] F. M. Cornford treats it as an argument of the sort by which Plato "skillfully masked" the conclusion that is meant to be accepted by the reader who thinks hard for himself.[6] A. E. Taylor is more favorably inclined toward the Anytos episode but unfortunately deals only glancingly with the main points which come under attack from other commentators.[7] More telling than the negative criticism is the neglect of the Anytos episode in comparison with other parts of the dialogue.

There are several signs that the Anytos episode is especially impor-

tant: it returns to the politico-historical setting which the opening of
the dialogue had set up as the key; Socrates accepts its finding without
reservation; and it is exceptionally long. We find in it a distinctive
political approach which is not developed elsewhere in Plato. It would
be inappropriate to discuss this, however, while the surface structure
of the argument is still in doubt. Hence in this chapter we examine the
argument closely, leaving to chapter 6 the broader significance of the
episode. Here we consider (i) the identification of the problem, (ii) its
logic or formal character, (iii) its content and (iv) its grounds.

(i)   Identification of the Problem

Socrates enlists first Anytos and then Meno to help him test the
earlier conclusion that virtue is teachable. In effect, the earlier argument is being criticized for not being in touch with hard facts. The
usefulness and knowledge attributed to virtue are generic, not peculiar to it. The treatment is thus pejoratively theoretical, since it provides no means of singling out the particular thing whose teachability
was being argued.

In the subsequent discussion which Socrates has with Anytos, on
the contrary, Socrates uses a notion of virtue which functions osten-
sively by naming the individuals who possess it, Themistocles, Aristides, and so forth. This notion is initially formulated as: "that wisdom and virtue whereby men manage houses and cities well and
honour their parents, and know how to entertain fellow-citizens and
strangers, and to speed them on their way, as a good man ought to do"
(91A–B—Lamb trans.). This formula improves on Meno's old definition since it topically covers the institutions and kinds of people with
whom one has actional relations and it qualifies the acts as those
which "a good man ought to do." Meno somewhat neglected both the
coverage and the qualification. But the new formula does not satisfy
the criteria Socrates had initially set up for a good definition. Rather, it
functions in this argument not as an object of inquiry but as a means of
directing Anytos' mind to the actual men whose practices are admired
as having been good in and for Athens, that is, to virtue-as-possessed.

The shift in emphasis from the earlier argument is from the universal in useful actions to the socio-historical conditions. In today's
terms, Plato's emphasis is on values as fact. But to say this is not
enough. B. F. Skinner similarly insists on treating values as facts, but
to him their objective status carries with it their susceptibility to
quantification or other systematic treatment.[8] For Plato here, this is an
unwarranted reduction. That values are facts does not predetermine
whether they can be systematized. The contrast is clear when we bear
in mind that Plato is talking not simply about virtuous acts but about

virtue as a power in men for producing them. Such powers are not reducible to schedules of acts. The powers can be identified when they appear and thus are themselves facts, and yet the possibility clearly remains that they are too open to be subsumed under universal concepts or theories and hence are not teachable.

To test for this possibility the inquirers, as we have noted, look at cases in Athens and Thessaly. These are the proper places to look because Socrates and Meno respectively have direct experience of the two cities. Conversely, the circumstantial reason for not including Spartan (or other) practices is that neither of the participants has the kind of concrete knowledge of them required here.

The question whether Anytos is needed in the dialogue at all raises the same issue. R. S. Bluck says that the argument could have "continued on much the same line without him."[9] Although it is true that Socrates is acquainted with the Athenian system, Anytos alone supplies a concrete case of the system's failure to teach, just as Meno supplies the same for Thessaly. They are part of the data they are surveying, as Socrates' introduction of Anytos makes clear in his case (89E–90B).

The nature of the problem being dealt with in the Anytos episode is set by the emphasis we have noted. The shift from the question of virtue as knowledge to actual cases of teaching means a shift from the question whether the teaching of virtue is possible to the question whether it exists. Even if virtue were known to be knowledge, a formulation of the knowledge would not itself be the relevant evidence. On the other hand, mere observation of one person who is talking to another about virtue is obviously inconclusive. Even the outcome in the student, though it is necessary evidence and is critical in the Anytos episode, is still not sufficient. All admit Pericles turned out to be virtuous, but that is not evidence he acquired his virtue from a teacher.

Consideration of results in possible learners must therefore be supplemented by evidence of the likelihood that putative teachers will do their best. When Anytos is asked whether Themistocles was a good teacher of virtue, he says, "In my opinion, yes, assuming that he wished to be so" (93C). They are considering men who besides professing or possessing virtue have intrinsic motivation to teach it—either for money and prestige or for virtuous sons.[10]

If men so motivated exist, and if the students turn out to be virtuous, then we have some assurance that the communication process which took place between them was in fact the transmission process—the middle link between their virtues. The argument shows, unfortunately, that there is no such process. We turn now to the logical character of that argument.

(ii)   *The Logic of the Argument*

a) The Anytos episode appears initially to be another hypothetical deductive argument, the major premise being the hypothetical statement that if virtue is teachable there must be teachers of it (89D). In effect the deduction from this is *modus tollens;* that is, there are no teachers, hence virtue is not teachable at all. But Socrates in fact uses the negative converse hypothesis, that if there are no teachers of virtue, virtue is not teachable (89E). The deduction from this is that virtue is not teachable; and this conclusion provides the basis for an implicit *modus tollens* inference from the original hypothesis that if virtue is knowledge it is teachable. The chain would then be: since no teachers, not teachable, and since not teachable, then not knowledge.

This chain has come under attack. Jacob Klein asserts that though concern with existent teachers involves a genuine political problem, the existence or nonexistence of teachers of virtue may not determine whether or not it is teachable.[11] Again, Victor Goldschmidt carries the doubt back to the first link in the chain, arguing that the nonexistence of teachers or learners of virtue is merely accidental and not of significance in determining the nature of virtue.[12]

Such attacks seem to be only incidentally directed to the logical form of the argument, and Klein is clearly right in noting the political context. We believe, however, that logical structure, meaning, and practical applicability are all brought into line with each other in the argument. Let us begin with a more careful scrutiny of the logic.

There is a significant difference between the positive and negative hypotheses. The positive is presented as necessary: if virtue is teachable, there must be (*anangkaion*) teachers (89D). The negative converse, on the other hand, is presented as a surmise or likeness (*eikazontes eikazoimen*—89E). Since the finding does turn out to be negative, the inference that virtue is not teachable is presumably nothing more than a surmise. The assignment of this status to the logical process seems appropriate; a single positive case could upset it and a statistical survey could not definitely establish that no such case would appear. Even for any given moment one cannot show a total absence of such cases.

Though Plato seems aware of the contingency in the negative hypothesis, he still does not treat it as suspect. Its reliability is supported, though certainly not guaranteed, by the inclusion within it of reference not only to the subject matter but to the mode of inference being made about it. The positive hypothesis does not do this; its reference is only to the subject matter. In asserting a necessary connection between teachability and teachers, it makes the former itself involve (if it does not entail) the latter. But the negative hypothesis cannot simply lay down an involvement, for the reasoning is from a nonexistence (no teacher) and concerns a non-relation. The nonexistence does not directly implicate or involve non-teachability; rather some mind must think or assert the negative claim. Thus the distinction between the positive and the negative hypothesis is not merely one between the statement of a necessary relation and the statement of a contingent relation, but between a necessity and an act of judgment. In the negative converse the act of inference explicitly makes the needed connection. If there are no teachers then "rightly surmising we may surmise," and so forth (89E). The surmise, or, in an alternative translation, the inference from likeness, is not in the subject matter. Introduction of this mental operation compensates for the dependence on negation.

b) One can also ask what the warrant is for the "necessity" of the positive hypothesis, that if virtue is teachable, there must be teachers of it. One could object to this hypothesis by pointing out that although solid geometry in the *Republic* is teachable, there are, as it happens, no teachers of it. The question is, What does "teachable" (*didakton*) mean as used here in the *Meno*?[13] We assume that the meaning must provide for the necessity in the positive hypothesis as applicable to the actual, not possible, teachers being sought in the Anytos episode as its culmination. Socrates indicates such a meaning in explaining the problem of the inquiry to Anytos: "Whether virtue is teachable; this has been our problem all the time. And our inquiry into this problem resolves itself into the question: Did the good men of our own and former times know how to transmit to another man the virtue in respect of which they were good, or is it something not to be transmitted (*paradonton*) or taken over (*paralēpton*) from one human being to another?" (93A–B). The question whether virtue is teachable, unlike the solid geometry which in *Republic* VII Socrates projects as teachable before it has in fact been developed, is bound up with whether it has been and is being taught. If the proposition were only a record of events it would not imply transmissibility. But to Socrates it does here ascribe that property. He assumes that the possibility of teaching a subject and the facts about its having been taught, are not independent of each other. This is consistent with the much earlier and even more fundamental assumption which we noted in chapter 2—that the mode of acquisition is assumed to be a part of the sort of entity it is here taken to be.

Thus the question is whether virtue falls among the existent things that are continued and perpetuated among men by teaching (Socrates explicitly generalizes the positive hypothesis to "all" things that are *didakton*—89D). Teachability or being taught is both an operational fact *and* an indefinitely extendable pattern. The merging of the two means saying that the teaching of virtue exists; indeed, such an expression properly bypasses the substance/property distinction. It is an enduring event. Similarly in the expression, "English spoken here," the speaking of it has an unambiguous temporal existence without particular temporal location. A political planner seeking to keep alive some valued human ability would be concerned first with whether that ability was among the things preserved and projected by teaching.

In this commonsense use of *didakton*, teachers are necessarily bound up with its meaning. Indeed, though the line of inference is from teachability to teachers, the direction of causation can plausibly begin with teachers. The conclusion—that there are teachers—obviously guarantees that there is teachability.

c) We have dealt thus far with the relations of elements in the argument. A corresponding question concerns the identifying of those who are teachers and those who are not. In section iv below we consider the experience and assumptions needed for right identifications. We restrict ourselves here to the relation of the judgment to the object judged so far as it turns on the kind of mental act involved. Verbs as different as "suppose" (*oiēthenai*—92D) and "know" (*eidenai*—91B) are used. More striking is the fact that such verbs, which apply more or less to the object identified, are less frequently used than words characterizing the competence of the judge as being wise or sensible (*sōphrōn*—90D) or as unreasonable or stupid (*alogia, amathia*—90E). The reason for this variety of uses is that the problem is not simply accuracy about the object (teacher). This problem, of course, is included, but only as an aspect of making a practical judgment. One normally speaks of the latter as sensible or foolish, but does not say this of a simply accurate or inaccurate identification of an object.

The sense in which the judgment in the Anytos episode is practical therefore goes well beyond earlier parts of the dialogue. In the major models of thought treated up to this point by Plato, cognitive acts are object-oriented. The Anytos episode is of course a sort of inquiry (*zētein*—90B). But Socrates immediately specifies the problem as that of giving advice to Meno on what to do. To identify a teacher in principle is to decide to send Meno to him. At first this actional focus is a mere literary device: "Consider it thus: if we wanted Meno here to be a good doctor, to whom would we send him?" (90C).[14] Then the question applies literally: "[Meno] has been declaring to me ever so long, Anytos, that he desires to have that wisdom and virtue. . . . Now tell me, to whom ought we properly send him for lessons?" (91B). When Socrates' suggestion of the sophists is rejected, he puts the problem more directly to Anytos as a good act: "I only ask you to tell us, and do Meno a service as a friend of your family by letting him know to whom in all this great city he should apply" (92D).[15] Similarly, the great men with sons are spoken of as having to make a practical judgment: Are there any men, whether they themselves or others, available to teach their sons?

In general, Socrates and Anytos are like persons identifying a good doctor in order to consult him rather than like the examiners who certify his knowledge. The former think in practical terms not only because they look to the acts of the doctor, but because they must make a choice, and this fact governs the judgment. Hence Socrates prefers the circumlocution, "we should be wise in sending Meno" (90D) to such and such a man, to the simple assertion that we know the man to be such and such.[16]

(iii)   The Content

We turn now to the subject matter of the argument, the search for teachers of virtue. It is quickly summarized. In an interchange with Anytos, Socrates concludes first that while various practitioners of the arts are teachers, the sophists and then the Athenian statesmen are not teachers of virtue, the latter because of their failure to teach their sons. Anytos is angered. A second interchange occurs when Socrates turns to Meno and finds that in Thessaly the gentlemen are confused about the teaching of virtue, that the orator Gorgias does not claim the power for sophists, and that the poet Theognis is ambivalent. Meno is bemused by the conclusion that virtue is not teachable.

The significance of this survey depends on both interchanges. Although Klein says that the interchange with Meno is an "epilogue summarizing what has been said and also touching on opinions of a poet,"[17] it is more nearly a coordinate part. It surveys Meno's Thessaly, thus going beyond the special situation in Anytos' Athens. More important, the two states together provide completeness in principle. As presented by both the opening of the dialogue and the Anytos episode, Athens appears with indications of her past glory and great leaders. The praise of Themistocles, Aristides, and Pericles suggests the imperial but also open and humanistic society celebrated in Pericles' funeral oration. But both the opening and the Anytos episode point also to the present decline of Athens, a decline marked by a hostile repressive attitude toward open moral and political discussion. Thessaly, on the other hand, is a state whose opulence and elitism have little substantive tie with individual or political virtue; but she is now marked by a surge of free sophistical discourse. The two states are near-inversions of each other; one is noted for the practice of virtue, the other for freedom of discourse about it. Sparta would be a less apposite city here because its static code and culture make it similar to the closed-in model of a technical art, although the fact that Spartans call a good man "divine" (99D) suggests their need for better guidance. Further, Athens and Thessaly are now both involved in social change. Athens' problem is what to do about the present falling-away from what she had achieved; that of Thessaly is to discover how to move from material elitist success to substantive values, how to find the basis for acquiring virtue.

Accordingly, the interchange with Anytos turns on existent abilities, while that with Meno turns on prescriptive formulations about them. In the former, Socrates begins by setting up some arts—medicine, cobbling, flute-playing—as models. The teacher is called here first by the same name as the practitioner ("physician"), and then this name is refined into a "professor" of the art. Although Anytos accepts this as a model, he refuses also to consider the sophists as teachers of virtue; his censures are directed less against the sophists than they are against the cities and relatives who make it possible for youths to go to the sophists (92B), thereby turning away from the Athenian *kaloi kagathoi*—gentlemen "who share certain traditional standards of conduct"[18]—as their guide (92E). When the argument declares that even the most eminent of these men cannot teach virtue, Anytos stalks off in anger; for him the future of Athens depends on the transmission of the virtues of such men.

The interchange with Meno, though concluding the same point, is radically different. Socrates even reverses the order of the Athenian survey, moving from the good men to the sophists to Theognis, with the latter's art being invoked as something revelatory rather than as a model. The good men are thus the least important, remaining unnamed (those named earlier, in the opening, are morally suspect); and in general the emphasis throughout is on what men say about teachability, not what they do. The question about good men is not whether they have taught anyone but whether they are willing to put themselves forward as teachers; and their confusion on this point is enough to dismiss them. The question about the sophists is not whether, like other professors, they have attracted many students but whether a preeminent sophist, Gorgias, says that they teach virtue. Their business, he says, is only to teach skill in speaking. Finally, Theognis at times gives the impression that virtue can be taught and at other times that it cannot.

Thus the two surveys are of different objects—one of the existence of virtue as teachable and the other of the formulation of virtue as teachable. These have different though convergent emphases. The difference is illustrated by the treatments of bad nature in a youth. In the first interchange the assumption is that if a youth were bad (*kakos*), then his not becoming virtuous would not show that virtue is not teachable. Assurance is given that Cleophantos was not bad by nature (93D). In the second interchange, however, Theognis cites the recalcitrance of a bad man as evidence that the father lacked the power to transmit virtue: " 'Could understanding be created and put into a man . . . Never would a bad son have sprung from a good father, for he would have followed the precepts of wisdom, but not by teaching wilt thou ever make the bad man good' " (95E–96A—Lamb, trans.).

The point of the first interchange is that good men cannot find prescriptions usable by even the most willing minds, for there are no clear directions on what to do. The point of the second is that the formulations or precepts of virtue even if implanted from infancy have no force for resistant minds—as if the value or imperative of virtue did not overcome the resistance.[19]

Thus, in sum, virtuous men may be said to lack a teachable system in the sense of a formulable set of rules and directive principle. The reason for the lack cannot be said to be the difference of this virtue from the rigor of, say, mathematics. It is true that virtue here deals with acts and decisions. But the contrast is not with mathematics but with a broad range of arts, including even wrestling, which nonetheless achieve enough order for cognitive transmission. The reason that wrestling is teachable is that its province is so limited—victory over one man by bodily force in accordance with agreed-on rules—that there are a number of useful guides which, like recipes, may be given to the student for dealing with various types of opponents and circumstances. Even when the artist is inventing techniques, the end of the art is sufficiently restricted for him to anticipate the likely success of the technique. When the result is successful, then the new technique he used becomes another rule of production. In that sense the end in view guides judgment. The concrete uniqueness of each bout of wrestling does not preclude a useful order of rules and directive principle from being built up within the narrow limits of the art.

Such limits are what is lacking in the case of virtue. Virtue and vice are involved in all acts. The ostensive "definition" of virtue, previously cited, is a total inventory system for social acts. The teaching of flute-playing no doubt falls under the flute-playing art; but the choosing to do so is a question of virtue. The difficulties of systematizing rules of virtuous action are not accounted for sufficiently by the multiplicity of the acts falling within virtue's province, however. The outstanding men of virtue in the Anytos episode are leaders of the state; the course of affairs they direct is theory-resistant as much because it is always in change as because it is complex.

The contrast with the other practical but teachable arts is thus fairly definite. But to round out the indications of the character of virtue the

Anytos episode needs a comparison between virtue and the sophists' art as well. In the case of Gorgias this is specifically rhetoric ("speaking well"—95C), which shares with politics the magnitude setting it off from the teachable arts. Rhetoric traditionally deals with any subject; and the first point Socrates makes about Gorgias is that the latter offers to answer any question whatever put by any Greek (70B–C). But both Gorgias' art and Protagoras' more practical variant of it are teachable. There are some ways of building an ordered system to deal with the expansive spread of these arts. The fact that men of political virtue do not do this is surely one reason for giving contrasting prominence here to sophistic arts. They show that some means for ordering the expansive spread is possible. But theirs is only verbal, providing the means of arguing on any side of an issue. The virtuous man's judgments and arts, however, are not thus variable. He lacks an art that can determine the right judgment for a case; but he does determine it rightly and definitely, and does so with regard to matters of the same scope which the sophists cover only verbally.

We cannot draw more specific characterizations of him from the text; but suggest that since the problems are of a sort on which there are right and wrong rather than merely controversial judgments of the scope indicated, an order of principles for them operates in some sense and warrants them. Certainly this order is beyond the intelligible grasp of men; but an act can be good for reasons other than the reasoning of the agent—though obviously the connection must be intimate. In Kant's terms, nature rather than the concept may here give the rule.[20] The structure of the Anytos episode encourages us to suppose also that nature draws the rule from a comprehensive system. In discussing the two interchanges of the episode, we saw that they lacked guides and a determinate directive value for the teaching of virtue. We also have now contrasted virtue with the arts in order to show that the episode explains this lack of reference to a broad context beyond man's intellectual grasp yet determinate enough (or sufficiently divine in origin) to prevent virtue's being variable.

(iv)   *The Grounds*

What are the grounds, the material bases, of the argument of the Anytos episode? We consider these first with respect to the model arts, then with respect to the sophists, and finally with respect to the good men and their sons.

The arts are models because teachable. Of course the argument does not proceed by directly examining the knowledge which makes them teachable. Rather the judgment that they are teachable rests on a public consensus evident in the success of the practitioners. The models which Socrates uses—medicine, cobbling, flute-playing—constitute a rational sequence not in kinds of skills but in effects on the consumer: health, utility, and pleasure.

The ground of the argument, however, is not simply public satisfaction. Such a satisfaction is obviously with the objects made—health, shoes, music—and follows a judgment according to a test of time.[21] Accordingly, there is a twofold implication about the nature of the arts to be drawn from the use of public consensus as the ground for determining their teachability. First, the criteria the artist uses to determine the nature and adequacy of his product do not derive from the assumption of a "pure," self-determining art but are worked out in adaptation to the consumer's responses. This social determination perhaps has the greatest role in flute-playing and the least in medicine, but it functions in all, and remains prominent throughout the Anytos episode. Second, since public judgments of the craftsman test him by his consistency in producing the same results over time, the objects made are knowable to the user, for they have a repeatable identity which signifies the maker's art. In short, while the public judges from interest in and need for action, the application of criteria provides signs about the object that are consonant with the art's being knowledge.

The sophists, exemplified by Protagoras and Gorgias and by the poet Theognis, are tested on this model for the teaching of virtue. They fall short in different ways, but how they do so contributes to the affirmative side of the Anytos episode. That is, although the argument establishes the negative proposition that virtue is not teachable, it proceeds throughout on the assumption that virtue exists and is identifiable. Theognis contradicts himself (though there is little doubt that the Socrates of the *Protagoras* interpreting Simonides could have reconciled the contradiction!); but the kind of "teaching" which he points to is of a sort which in fact is consistent with the dialogue's later conclusion that virtue is right opinion. "Teaching," for Theognis, takes places when the student is simply in the presence of good men of power; and their discourse, allied with the exercise of virtue, would bring the hearer as close as possible to direct contact with it. Gorgias' art is teachable, but it is only the art of speaking well. His embellishments of virtue are remote from the problem of making policy. Nonetheless the subject matter is still virtue and the success of his teaching makes the verbal constructs a common social possession. Though these speeches have nothing to do with specific policy, their concern with general verbal values is the sign of some real common values, since the audience has to accept the latter, regardless of how tentatively or superficially, and this is a condition for the appeal of the embellishments. Isocratean epideictic rhetoric also illustrates this point.

Protagoras is treated here as closer to the problem of action. There is not a full consensus on him; Anytos has ill will toward him, but Socrates emphasizes Protagoras' thoroughly time-tested success. Even when one supposes that Protagoras' art is that of acquiring self-serving advantages, both its "teachableness" and Socrates' respect for it in this operationist context are plausible. Though the objective may be only to show how one can maintain the appearance of obedience to the law whatever the facts, law is in that sense being accepted. This use of law both makes that art teachable, and gives the rule of law the kind of value Protagoras sets forth in this myth in *Protagoras*. This acceptance, which is the minimal feature of such sophistry, can be expanded more respectably, but on the same principle, into a teaching of generalized constitutional theory as the basis of social achievements. Thus in Theognis,[22] Gorgias, and Protagoras the evidence that virtue is not teachable is still accompanied by signs of the presence of the social practices and thought compatible with the affirmative assumption that virtue really does exist.

Though Socrates does not accept Anytos' intemperate repudiation of Protagoras, he does yield to him so far as the search for a teacher of virtue is concerned. In yielding, however, he is only acting consistently with his earlier statement, on seeing Anytos, that Anytos "is the sort of man to whom one may look for help" (90B). There are other remarks welcoming Anytos' assistance in the search. Even if we think these ironic we may presume Anytos to represent a strand of public opinion relevant to the judgment of virtuous men in Athens. He was raised by a good father; if virtue were teachable, he would be good, one presumes; and both he and the Athenians think he is, though we are to understand that he is not, since here there appears in him evidence of the beliefs and attitudes which led to his prosecution of Socrates. There is a reason why Anytos can mistake himself for a statesman whom an inquirer who depends on public opinion (as Socrates does in the Anytos episode) would want to attend to. Anytos' life is wrapped up in the mores, values, and heroes of Athens. We agree with A. E. Taylor that Anytos is an able and public-spirited man to the measure of his intelligence, simply reflecting common Athenian attitudes.[23] He may not know Athens, but he is *of* her through and through. This makes it reasonable for him to say that it is not the sophists who are mad, only those who enable the young to go to them. Anytos can feel that the Athenian young and their parents should have some sense of what is alien to Athens. This trait in them he can "know" without experience of the sophists, who have no role in the community. The alternative to these sophists as candidates for teachers is "any Athenian gentleman" (92E). Socrates ironically calls Anytos a prophet (*mantis*)—but he calls genuinely good men of Athens by the same epithet (99D). It seems clear, then, that Plato's operationist mode in this episode sets up Athens as an object which, while it has not the simple time-tested repeatability of shoemaking, serves as the concrete base of the argument. This suggestion is then filled out in the judgments made of good men and their sons, and there are no disagreements about them.

To take an extreme but symptomatic example, when Socrates wants to show that Cleophantes was not good, he does so by asking, "But . . . did you ever hear anybody, old or young, say that [he] . . . had the same goodness and accomplishments of his father?" (93E). An agreement so rooted in so many men's opinions again suggests repeatable objects or some kind of stable base. Anytos, as we saw, treats Athenian gentlemen as undifferentiable for this purpose.

This stability is not undermined by the sharp differences among the great individuals next considered—Themistocles, Aristides, Pericles, and Thucydides—who paired as opposites in successive periods. Nothing is made of these differences. All the men alike are good, having a political virtue in some way the same. In this context the differences, taken for granted though unmentioned, would be plausible marks of the political ability needed for the guidance of Athens. One can indeed construct four phases of Athenian growth and greatness in terms of the key elements in the popular reputations of the four leaders: the preservation of the state in repulsing the Persians: the concern for justice domestically and in the Delian confederacy; the achievement of cultural and imperial hegemony; and a wise conservatism in using Athens' power and resources. Like the four presidents on Mt. Rushmore, each man was right for the need he met in the flowering of the nation, and it seems evident both that the first three represent especially important elements in that growth, and that Aristides and Pericles in their humanistic leadership transcend the self-interest of Athens.[24] In this sense the range of these leaders reinforces the signs of the argument that we noted above, of a quasi-repeatable identity grounded in Athens itself. This identity, rather than Platonic ideas, provides the achievements which the virtue of new leaders should sustain and extend.

This concludes our analysis of the Anytos episode. We have seen that the operationism envisaged in the opening of the dialogue and made progressively more necessary and relevant by the progress of the argument reaches a culmination here. Reliance on the opinion of the many, immersion in the immediate situation of Athens and Thessaly, characterizing as good the same politicians who are censured in the *Gorgias*—these are signs of a new kind of Platonic realism. Socrates is realistic in the *Gorgias*, of course, when he tells Callicles that the latter's belief in the law of the jungle.is what most men really think but will not say. But the realism of the Anytos episode is operationist in ignoring the secret, nonoperative, hidden beliefs of men in favor of the moral canons and judgments to which men will openly commit themselves and upon which they will act. We have not sought in this chapter to develop the broader nature of this realism, but have restricted ourselves to showing that the argument is no mere expression of contempt for Anytos and Meno but rather a tightly-structured, deliberate inquiry producing a reliable refutation of the preceding abstract argument that virtue is teachable. On this basis we are now in a position to move, in chapter 6, to the nature of the approach and to the political outlook it sets up as practicable for such states as Athens and Thessaly.

6   The Anytos Episode B: The
Economics of Virtue

Embedded in the arguments of the Anytos episode (examined in chap. 5) are political processes which themselves are underpinned by a theory of action and of associated cognitive states developed in the final portion of the dialogue (96D–100C—see chap. 7). Accordingly we consider here the politico-historical situation and the conception that virtue is primarily political. We emphasize the operationist approach which Socrates worked out to apply to available statesmen and immediate conditions rather than to an ideal, and the practical value of the approach as therefore suitable in particular for the problems and needs of Meno's Thessaly and Anytos' Athens, including the import of Socrates telling Meno to carry the final conclusion to Anytos. To deepen the perspective, comparisons are made both with the virtue of Athenian statesmen in other Platonic dialogues and with alternative conceptions in Greek philosophy and rhetoric.

(i)   *What Virtue Has Become*

In contrast with the *Republic*, in which the justice of the state is the same as that of the individual both by analogy and by interaction, the

Meno, at critical points, distinguishes social from individual virtue. The distinction does not emerge in the section on definition, but when the inquiry runs into trouble, the slave-boy episode is set up to concentrate exclusively on the internal and individual (self-moving) resources of the person. Inquiry so based is presented as the road to being better, braver, and less helpless (86B). In the hypothetical argument Socrates, concerned with consequences, implicitly reintroduced the social dimension, but the consequence he made explicit was the happiness brought about by guidance of the soul (88C). When this runs into difficulty, so that the empirical test of the Anytos episode is needed (as we noted in chap. 5), he makes the full turn to the social with virtue conceived now independently, or at least discussed without reference to the powers and properties of the soul.

There are two steps in this turn. His first consists in the ostensive "definition" cited earlier, that is, the "wisdom and virtue whereby men manage their house or their city well,'' and so forth (91A), an identification in terms of consequences realized in external relations. As the second step Socrates drops the full inventory which the definition gave of institutions and persons on whom the good man acts, and isolates the political. The concern is with men good at things political (*agatha ta politika*—93A); and this virtue is not further analyzed but is taken as it exists in historical statesmen. The "definition" directed Anytos' mind to them and hence not to a concept of virtue but to a virtue as it is possessed by actual public figures.

Such an emphasis on leadership reinforces the separating of the conception of virtue from the nature of the individual. The managerial excellence is the same as that used in households; the same verb is used to describe both—*diokein* (91A). As the verb indicates, it is an economic steering, and we may reasonably infer its concern with the material and moral resources, the rights and duties on which the pursuit of happiness depends. In the *Republic* V, Plato works with an analogy between state and family, but in a way different from that of the *Meno*. In the *Republic* the emphasis is on the unity of the family-state as embodying its pattern of love. In the *Meno*, the state is not presented as embodying a pattern but as maintaining itself; statesmen keep the state upright (*orthousin*—99C).

Virtue is thus excellence in social administration, not in determining the ends of individuals. Individuals or groups as private make this determination themselves—it is an open society. However, the social administration is not thereby value-free. The leaders' efficacy consists in preserving attained values and in assuring to men conditions of opportunity for the free determination and achievement of further values both private and public. So conceived, the function of statesmen is not morally prescriptive but—we can say this without paradox—nonetheless requires their moral leadership.

Our interpretation of this part of the dialogue is supported by the way Socrates uses arts as models for politics in the *Meno* in contrast with the way he does in the *Gorgias* (501D463–66). In both dialogues, medicine is a paradigm. But they treat flute-playing in opposite ways. In the *Meno*, it is analogous to medicine, while in the *Gorgias*, it exemplifies irrational pursuits. In the *Gorgias*, medicine is rational because it has a determinate subject matter; flute-playing is rather a knack of giving pleasure, and thereby flattering the listener. This pleasure, not grounded in reason, has the pseudocognitive effect of making the listener think that he is in good condition, imitating the way medicine really puts the body in good condition. In the *Meno*, on the other hand, the ground for saying that medicine is an art is that it is taught. So is flute-playing. The analogy then, is fairly easy to establish. The flute-playing of the *Meno* would be treated in terms not of the cognitive import of pleasure but rather of the restorative effect of that pleasure—of its tendency, like that of medicine, to set the listener upright, renewing him for the activities of a (virtuous) life.

The value-conditional or instrumental character of social virtue makes sense of the *Meno*'s reliance on the good opinion of the many to identify good men. Public confidence is essential to leadership in an open society, and the statesman's possession of this confidence indicates his attunement to existent interests and their possibilities. Statesmen are characterized by *eudoxia*, which indicates good repute as well as good opinion. Acquiring eudoxia in the *Meno*, unlike the *Gorgias* or the *Crito*, does not make the character of the leader suspect. The reason for the difference is not merely that the dialogues assess reputation differently. In the *Crito*, Socrates turns away from the opinion of the many because it is random. We have already noted how in the *Meno* the opinions of the public he seeks are not random but are time-tested; they have remained unchanged and have had a long succession of like objects to judge. Public judgment here is not of the statesman's "pure" values, such as the refusal to requite injury with injury, but of what the many are capable of judging reasonably well and firsthand, that is, the utility of diverse social circumstances for working out their problems of living well. Of course their judgment of a given policy at a given time is often faulty, but not their judgment of a leader's general ability as tested by a good number of policies over time and constituting a program; and this is the concern of the *Meno*.

This context makes it understandable that public opinion could be divided on the sophists and that Socrates could show them considerable respect, yet would yield to Anytos' dismissal of them. The sophists do offer a set of tools for dealing with whatever turns up—a sort of readiness. The similarity to social-managerial virtue is close, but with the exception that the sophists' tools are means of achieving whatever one pleases rather than of promoting individual virtue. Yet the latter is not altogether precluded.

Comparison With the Treatment of Virtue in Other Dialogues

It will be useful here to set off the *Meno*'s treatment of Athenian politicians from similar Platonic treatments in the *Laches* and the *Phaedrus*. The same statesmen are praised as in the *Meno*: Pericles in the *Phaedrus*, Aristides and Thucydides in the *Laches*. Indeed, the problem in the *Laches* at first seems to be identical with that of the Anytos episode: all agree on the presence of virtue in the fathers and the lack of any special merit in the sons. The problem here is how to teach it to the grandsons. Since in some respect the "same" virtue is being talked about as that of the *Meno*, the direction the *Laches* takes is novel. Socrates suggests that they forego any attempt to say what the whole of virtue is and consider instead their knowledge of a part (190C); and when it turns out that a knowledge of courage must involve a knowledge of the whole, this connection is taken to mark the failure of the inquiry. In the *Meno* the whole-part relation is reversed from that of the *Laches*; in the *Meno* explanations in terms of justice or courage are rejected because they provide only a part before the whole is at hand.

The difference goes back to the fact that, whereas the *Meno* conceives virtue in terms of external effects, the *Laches* deals with virtue as the property which activates what by analogy would be the native capacity of man; sight is to virtue as the eye is to man: "If we happen to know that sight joined to eyes makes the eyes the better for it, and further, if we are able to get it joined to eyes, we obviously know what this faculty of sight is, on which we might be consulting as to how it might be best and most easily acquired" (189E–190A—Lamb, trans.).

From this analogy the *Laches* would properly attend to courage, it being the virtue by which man actualizes himself as a force in the community. The acquiring of courage in the *Laches* is a condition of action and in that sense it would be a first step in the self-determination of the individual. The part here thus comes before the whole, serially, though a man would also need to keep his eye on the outcome. Socrates describes the consultative situation within the dialogue as one in which the discussants do know what virtue is (190B–C) yet would find it "easier" to identify a part of it (190C). When Callicles in the *Gorgias* takes courage as primary, he seeks to make it all-encompassing, whereas the participants in the *Laches* consider courage to be part of virtue and no more.

The peculiarity of the *Meno*, first set up in the section on definition, is that on the one hand contact with virtue as a whole, nothing less, is being sought, while on the other Socrates supposes that nothing at all, not even the least thing, is known about virtue (71A). The assumption thus is that the barest minimum of genuine acquaintance depends upon acquaintance with the whole. Although no definition satisfies this requirement, the later conception of virtue as social-managerial, though at a different level, does provide just this minimum-whole contact. It must encompass the city to make available the conditions for the development of the virtue and happiness of all. At the same time, as not determinative of those ends, it would require only the least and initial contact with the values thus made possible. In sum, while the *Laches* treats of what today would be called a stage in the individual's establishing of his identity, the whole being its ultimate filling-out, the *Meno* is concerned with the state's provision of the conditions under which such fulfillment can occur.

The *Phaedrus* provides a different counterpoint to the *Meno*, for in it Pericles is set in opposition to ordinary rhetoricians and is accordingly praised (269A–B, E). His study with Anaxagoras makes his concept of unity dialectical. We may accordingly presume his speeches are concerned with the whole state, and since the dialectical rhetorician is here centered on love, we may also believe that they make Athens an object of love for the community. Pericles' virtue is rhetorical. The Periclean social-managerial virtue of the *Meno*, on the other hand, lays down policies and shapes circumstances more directly and is concerned with the whole as the existential sum of opportunities and conditions open to all. As presented in the *Phaedrus*, Pericles could cause his audience to feast their eyes on Athens, and to be seduced by a great speech such as the funeral oration which the historian, Thucydides, presents. The *Meno* audience would make the judgment that they could live well and be led by a statesman with policies enabling them to do so; *this* audience would be the listeners, not to the funeral oration, but to the speeches on the conduct of war and of domestic life during the course of war.

Thus, while the virtue of the *Phaedrus* and the *Meno* both apply to the whole of Athens, that of the *Meno* is factual as contrasted with the dialectical ascent of the *Phaedrus*; and while the virtue of the *Laches* and the *Meno* alike is something to be acquired as the way to individual fulfillment, that of the *Meno* is a disposition in the leader to provide the bases for this fulfillment by all citizens as contrasted with the individual-stage development of the *Laches*. Finally, the Pericles of the *Gorgias* fails because none of the several virtues we have reviewed is connected directly to the primary Socratic task, illustrated in the slave-boy episode, of internally generating a development of the individual.

The juxtaposition of these dialogues eliminates the need for reconciling literally different statements among them, and helps isolate the peculiar concern of the *Meno* in the light of the comparison. The activities of Athenian statesmen obviously have many aspects, and one dialogue can center on one aspect, another on another. Thus the statesmen have their impact on the times (*Laches*); promote the sense of community based on an idealization of Athens as a unity (*Phaedrus*); set policies which nourished freedom of discourse in coexistence with institutions dependent on consent (*Meno*); and nonetheless cannot halt the corruption of Athenian life (*Gorgias*). And each problem generates the principles required for its solution. Thus, love in the *Phaedrus* is not merely a property of life but the principle of all souls (and they, of all motion); the source of cognition derived from it is verisimilitude. The corresponding point for us is that in the *Meno* managerial virtue is given its chance to be architectonic. It is the business of the gods, and the cognitive model for it is conceptual inquiry (recollection) because the advancement of knowledge depends on external conditions supplied by the capacities of certain men to be good managers.

(iii)   *The Politics of Leadership*

The basic fact about political virtue in the Anytos episode is its non-teachability. The difference between Socrates and Anytos on this question shows the advantages of Socrates' position. Anytos feels that the denial of teachability defames Athens' famous statesmen. He identifies their practical ability with knowledge, believing that what they can do they must know. Themistocles could certainly teach virtue if he wished (93C). Anytos extends his claims without limit: *Any* Athenian gentleman could teach Meno. Since these men do not, in fact, employ or possess a didactic theory, the effect of Anytos' position is that at the level of discourse, the "concepts" which the statesmen cite as the basis of policy—patriotism, tradition, duty, loyalty—take on the status of "knowledge"; and at the practical level the significance which these concepts supposedly have, makes loyalty to them the essence of the good life or something like it.

Like Anytos, Socrates begins by accepting the existence of virtuous men. He separates that, however, from the question of whether they possess the theory and, on the basis of his factual inquiry, decides that they do not. On the contrary, to ascribe a didactic theory to them would for Socrates be to defame them, in the sense obviously of committing them to more than they can achieve, that is, to transmit their own virtue and to set a model for what the complete good life is.

In summary, Anytos begins with a significant truth, which incidentally Meno misses, that is, the virtue of Athens' leaders and the state's dependence on them. But seeing nothing else, he extends this into unwarranted claims whose vulnerability accounts, in part, for his insecurities and the repressive impulses which he manifests in the exchange with Socrates. Socrates' position has the great advantage not only of fitting the facts but also of enabling him to give full recognition to the significant power of the statesmen and at the same time to take into account their limitations.

The inability to teach is only one form of the limitation to which the statesmen are subject. The cognitive restriction of their virtue to opinion or inspiration precludes their making an adequate analysis of the bases of their actions. It is, for one thing, not stable enough (only knowledge abides—97E). The same point, in other language, is that the virtue which the statesmen exercise is an operational principle itself undergoing modification as its exercise modifies the situation on which they act.

Recognition of the statesmen's limitation has advantages. The limitation is harmful only if there is a genuinely efficacious theoretic norm exhaustively covering the situation. But if there is not, the picture alters radically. The statesmen themselves become uniquely crucial to the state, for they rather than a mere theory are directive of it. The *Meno* suggests that their not being bound by an antecedent theory enables them to cope with contingencies, to provide for the unexpected, and in general to generate the guiding principles needed for the indeterminate conditions they face.

Such capacities constitute their virtue, and, as we have noted, it has two main features. The first is its scope, embracing no less in fact than the sophist's art does in words and determining proximate consequences for the whole state and distantly envisaging ultimate ends. The second is the capacity to maintain a broad-gauged historical continuity of virtuous acts building and extending Athenian tradition. This need not be a repetition of traditional forms or rules, but is a growth or maintenance of the state in simultaneously complex and temporally changing circumstances; the achievements of Themistocles, Aristides, Pericles, and Thucydides were each different in kind, but their political virtue as we have described it kept them responsive to the always-moving course of events. It is difficult to conceive of a fixed science that could have generated their decisions.

Now to corollaries of this conception of virtue.

a) Virtue is an acquisition in the radical sense that its content is added to a man from without. He does not awaken a disposition or idea latent in himself but absorbs values embedded in the social setting. If the state mirrored the individual or embodied a pattern, then recollection or something like it would be necessary. But in the state envisaged here the individual does not have to meet such a requirement. At the same time Plato has safeguards against the limitations of such operationism:to acquire externally-derived values is not a simple cultural relativism treating the individual as drawing his own ends from the social context, as with Anytos, who would no doubt think of the good man as the good citizen. For Socrates, the ends of the individual still depend on internal powers and reflection (the slaveboy episode). The values he draws from the social context include the larger ends of the state which he conceives as providing the external conditions for an individual's organization of his life.

b) The cognitive content of virtue is inseparable from its use, that is, the meaning of a statement of policy or a political principle is inseparable from the way it actually works. Because the existing state is indeterminate, there is no measure or test of the possession of virtue except in the consequences of action. This is the operationist side and it is basic. But virtue is not reducible to a pragmatic skill (Meno's error). It is not enough for a statesman to conceive and work for desired consequences. As divinely inspired, he works from an internal though shadowy vision of the whole state from which consequences are projected and continually reassessed in action. (This confirms most of the points being made here—that we have a political operationism but one in which the influence of the philosopher adds a significant dimension—that is, here the inspiration, by internalizing and grounding the pragmatism, provides a working substitute for a teleological principle.)

c) We have concentrated on the virtue of statesmen. What of the people generally? This is not a question of their private virtue as against the public virtue of politicians, but of the public virtue of both. The effectiveness of leadership in Athens depends on consent, and if this were determined only by the self-interest of individuals and groups, there would be no public virtue in them. Neither would the state be stable. The same public virtue is needed in all, but directively in leaders and responsively in citizens. Socrates neither presses the point nor does he bypass it. Anytos says any Athenian gentleman can teach the goodness being sought (92B); Socrates agrees that indeed there are many good Athenians and mentions the leaders as exemplars of political virtue. The conclusion we have drawn from this, as well as from the Anytos episode as a whole, is that the public virtue of citizens is the primary object and goal of the statesman's art—an economic art of providing for the maintenance of public virtue as itself the condition of and perhaps the stimulus to the pursuit of the best ends open to them as individuals.

(iv)   *The Politics of Virtuous Leadership in Comparison*
        with Other Theories

The treatment of virtue in the *Meno* marks a distinctive achievement
in Greek thought regarding the relativity of political processes. In the
large, the *Meno* stands between the rhetoricians and sophists, on the
one hand, and the naturalists or theoreticians on the other—with
Protagoras and Isocrates exemplifying the former and Aristotle and
Plato's *Republic* the latter. Protagoras and Isocrates were no more
identical than Aristotle and Plato's *Republic*, but we bypass differences here which are not needed for our purpose of locating the
distinctive character of the *Meno*'s treatment. The latter indicates how
a leader works well, but the critical point is that the state's working
well depends simply on his doing so; hence the politics of leadership.
Further, the absence of a theory of the state is what makes leadership
so central. It is true, as Karl Popper says, that Plato's *Republic* is
dependent entirely on its rulers, and he refers to this as his theory of
leadership.[1] The irony is that the leaders in the *Meno* do not have the
authority that those in the *Republic* have. The talent of our statesmen
in the *Meno*—eudoxia—must reflect public opinion, and it works by
guidance. Yet the statesmen in the *Meno* are more truly principles of
the state and determinants of its welfare than are the philosophers of
the *Republic*, since the latter apply their philosophic education while
the former must create for themselves, as our analysis has shown.
What we have called their limitation is imposed by the shifting situation they deal with, and this limitation thus becomes an essential part
of the virtue required in an open society. The result is that they can be
great leaders without being authoritarians.

Aristotle may provide a more illuminating contrast since he is
trying to solve problems rather than build a utopia. For him there is a
political science, though it is not a theoretical science. The scientific
character of his *Politics* is just the reason that Aristotle's *Rhetoric* is
constructed as the art of *ad hoc* decision-making. The rhetorician is not
a true politician, even if rhetoric is an ethical branch of politics.[2] The
rhetorician who thinks he is a politician is for Aristotle merely postur-
ing. The *Meno*, with its conception of leaders, takes a middle ground
between these two. The leaders are not merely constitutionalists on
the one hand nor, on the other, rhetoricians using an art of pro and con
to deal *ad hoc* with particulars. Rather they are men exercising a stable
disposition of the state in coping with particulars to preserve and
extend its continuity. Right opinion is not some characteristic of each
policy taken separately, but is rather a property of a kind of man. It is a
tendency to act in a certain way, to make successive decisions that are

good individually and that hold up together in the long run. This is indicated in the *Meno*'s concern to find virtuous men, not single right policies.

These leaders do have much in common with the rhetoricians and sophists. But there are critical differences. The politics of the *Meno* recognizes a region outside its own sphere which is theoretically adequate. The existence of this conceptual realm also opens up the possibility for the ends of life to be set outside the sphere of the political as such. (Isocrates certainly makes great men central to the welfare of the state, but he allows for no separate realm of theory. Astronomy is merely mental gymnastics, good as a preparation for rhetoric. Hence the good life for Isocrates is participation in the exercise of political virtue.) Another important difference of the *Meno*'s approach from that of the rhetorician is perhaps a subtle one, for it makes Protagoras' conception of man the measure more pertinent. Where in a given approach theoretical and practical disciplines are separate as in Aristotle or in the *Meno*, and where politics is accordingly in a territory apart from the theoretical, nonetheless the coexistence of the two in the approach as a whole has its effect. In Aristotle, this is obvious in the way in which political theory is modeled on natural science. In our next chapter, we will show a comparable modeling in the *Meno*, even if we need not call on that here to differentiate the rhetoricians in the politics of leadership itself. We have noted that while consequences are the final basis of judgment, pragmatism alone is not adequate. Though man may be unable to gain knowledge of the larger scheme of reality which warrants the inspiration he gets for a particular action (and hence the sophists' large schemes are not grounds of virtue), yet the pattern is nonetheless real, as suggested by the origin of man's virtue in the gods.[3] In the rhetorical conception of man the measure, there is no room for that larger scheme and for the definite rightness that it gives to the particular action.

By way of a supplement to the preceding, let us add that another achievement of the *Meno* is its capacity to account easily for the very many considerations involved in any action reaching the point of consent which makes it an established policy. One is deciding not merely on the policy but also on the man who proposes it and on the man who is to execute it. Often the vote is for the man rather than the policy, in which case the nexus is still more complex. Further, a policy is bound up with a scheme of priorities for the whole state and involves ongoing trends. There is no structure covering all factors involved in a policy or covering even the meaning of the words that formulate a policy. The *Meno*'s solution to the problem of grasping this complexity is certainly not an ideal one, but it may be the best there is, that is, to locate the center in the citizens seen in their capacities as guides and guided.

(v)   *Application to Thessaly and Athens*

Let us look at the application of this to Thessaly and Athens. Thessaly is enjoying its prosperity and horsemanship, and in the security of this affluence is engaging in the luxury of sophistic discourse. Athens is in decline (70E–71A) and is represented by an Anytos who is intent on holding on by discouraging or even suppressing what appears to be dissent. To a limited extent we may mark out modern counterparts of these two tendencies: the self-assured elitism of technological and industrial management, and the superpatriotism of political leaders who see traitors or misfits in dissenters.

These conditions are briefly shown in Socrates' speech at the opening about the two states; they are revealed further in the Anytos episode. The difficulties they show are inherent in the situation because virtue is *not* teachable. Nonetheless the *Meno* avoids the easy path of simply locating the resultant misrule in some tyrannical nature of rulers, as in the thirst for power in Thrasymachus or the outright evil of Archelaus. Self-interest and the desire for power are of course at work. But they do not explain enough or they oversimplify the practical problem.

The *Meno* shows us how both virtue itself and men's impulses toward it set up the difficulties. Meno is attracted to the praise of virtue but this has turned into a verbal diversion and so has left him in the dark about virtue. Anytos is immersed in surroundings which do have values he can sense without actually knowing; but his mistaking that sensing for knowing closes his mind. That Socrates recognizes that the difficulties begin with an attraction to virtue comes out in his indulgence of Meno and in his recruitment of Anytos in the search for teachers.[4]

The immediate practical needs which follow from these tendencies are to bring Meno into some awareness of what virtue is and to make Anytos tractable. The dialogue speaks to these needs by showing that virtue is good opinion coming as divine inspiration. It is true that Anytos is bound to be displeased by this, since he does not wish to find limitations to the powers of the Athenian leaders.[5] The image of these leaders who are operating from emotional seizures without understanding obviously cannot show them as explicitly sure of their grounds. Nevertheless the presentation that is made comes closer than could any other Socratic statement to satisfying Anytos and at the same time relaxing his impulse to repression. Socrates' notion of eudoxic guidance does elevate the virtues of the leaders and even gives them a higher certification. In comparison with the statements in the *Gorgias* or the *Apology* about political leaders, the conclusion of the *Meno* is an appeasement of Anytos. He would only need to recognize that Athens' welfare does not rest on a teachable orthodoxy. This could enable him to see how Socratic questioning is compatible with a full appreciation of Athens' achievements and leaders, for we have seen that the recognition of their intellectual limitations does not impugn the values they advance nor their merits in so doing. The "message" of the dialogue could mollify Anytos without transforming him. Socrates is showing that his position is no threat to the man; the immediate benefit that would come to Athens from Anytos' resultant security presumably could be that he would not prosecute Socrates. The dialogue ends on this note.

Although Socrates has angered Anytos, he now succeeds, up to a point, with Meno. The probable reasons for the difference are instructive. Meno, unlike Anytos, is not suspicious of intellectuals as such. The likely causes for this are that Gorgias is eager to please, that affluent Thessalian aristocrats feel secure, and there is no intellectual challenge to the low level of virtue in the leadership there. Nevertheless, even the idle discourse of Gorgias in praise of virtue does provide Socrates with a point of entry. Gorgias has stimulated an admiration of the poets as having powers clearly different from skill in riding and ruling. Socrates' conclusion at the end of the dialogue that virtue comes from divine inspiration sets up an immediate similarity to the poetic, and at least would carry for Meno a sense of a difference in virtue from skills measurable by their efficiency, such as wealth-getting. The concern of outstanding leaders with the whole fabric of the state and with men as interdependent would account for this difference, though Meno admittedly would not be aware of it in these terms. But it could be involved in his sense of the difference between divinely "poetic" virtue and acquisitive activities conceived as directed mainly to individual aggrandizement or gain. To put this in modern terms, Socrates has used this point of entry provided by interest in discourse about virtue to undermine any sense that Meno may have had that the kind of leader the state needs is a good businessman. In any event, an incipient sense of the difference is thus turned toward a sense of what virtue is—even apart from having it. This sense shows the insufficiency of taking Gorgias as a master and the need to study and to appreciate the actual leaders in the history of a great state. Socrates, quite shrewdly in the Anytos episode, adopts the device of asking Anytos to whom they should send Meno; and in this connection Theognis' utterance that one can learn much by spending time with good men of power makes sense; Pericles said that Athens was the school of Hellas.

Why is Meno the emissary whom Socrates chooses to carry the message of the dialogue to Anytos? The problem is basically to quiet Anytos' fears for the security of his position and also, presumably, for Athens' internal "law and order." To do this is hardly the business of a torpedo fish. Meno is as suitable an intermediary as one could get. He is receptive to the discourse of Socrates, and possessed of the power, station, and ambitions to carry weight with Anytos. While such a rhetorical mission is outside Socrates' own purview, the fact that he would attempt to bring it about is a sign of the orientation of the dialogue toward *ad hoc* correctives. Socrates' management here would exploit Meno's sophistry for possible improvement of his discourse and would use Anytos' respect for Meno and his admiration of Athenian leaders to raise the level of his tolerance of discourse. Meno is the right emissary because he points the meaning of the message to discourse.

In terms of Plato's *Republic*, this marks a roundabout attack on political repression. A much better means of insuring freedom would be to build and maintain a good state with a harmonious structure. But how is freedom maintained in existing societies? They are necessarily in a revolutionary situation, for even when there is little change, stability does not come from the natural adaptation of every element to its function but rather by the statesman's use of devices of power and policy to cope with the many variable impulses to change. Obviously the sources of the impulses to change lie mainly in men's pursuit of their particular interests; but correlated with this are notions about the political processes. The fact that virtue is not teachable will always generate, as it did with Meno, some scepticism about whether there exists any guidance genuinely concerned with the welfare of the whole state. Again, there are the natural recalcitrants, as Theognis indicates. The *Meno* concentrates, however, on the conditions inhibiting freedom of discourse, either by punishing its expression, as Anytos does, or restricting its pertinence, as the sophists do. Such conditions cannot be dealt with by praising freedom; indeed that, taken by itself, would be to repeat the mistake of the sophists.

(vi)   *Discourse and the Acquisition of Virtue*

The ultimate political question raised by the *Meno* is then the nature and function of discourse in politics. As non-didactic, it is a discourse of guidance, working by the interaction of leadership and public judgment and consent. Its immediate function is in establishing policy; over time it shows those among active public figures who have the "gift" of virtue. One hopes especially that it enables the youths capable of receiving the gift to discover this in themselves and to manifest it and be identified by society. In guidance-politics the continuity of leadership, and indeed of the state's stability, depend on such functions of discourse.

But the proper character of the discourse is not easy to pin down. The absence of a determinate or independent theory means that intellectual discourse as such lacks a constant ground and method; nor can this difficulty be resolved by restricting the concern of participants to immediate issues of policy; for the meaning of a policy statement depends inevitably on what connections it has with what broad ideas and political structure. We are in regions of opinion of a kind that are in danger of being caught in paradox: the concept of consent can ground dictatorial powers. Conversely, a literal rule against this can catastrophically prevent emergency action. The Anytos episode does not purport to offer answers to such difficulties, but combined with the ending of the dialogue it does point in a hopeful direction. It of course relates ideas and facts (the nature of teachers and their existence), but this is ordinary use, not some systematic "concrete universal." Rather, the key to method here is to render great social achievements as themselves the center of attention, the concrete "theory" on which to ground discourse. True, one does not derive the same universals or system of them from various historical successes. One reads off a far different rule of action from the Athenians' throwing themselves into their ships at Salamis, risking all, than from Pericles' caution at the beginning of the Peloponnesian War. Useful discourse here does not rise above the differences. On the contrary, the tendency is to keep the extrapolated rules bound up inseparably in meaning and "lesson" value with the original deed itself—this latter drawing significance from its relation to the state's position and possibilities at the time. Though they are and at some point are seen as fairly definite, their full recognition depends on open discourse, with its interplay of formulations and outlets for insight. This discourse of exemplary achievement works best when applied in freedom to the speaker's native state but has to draw as well on the best that man has said or done.

The same considerations apply to the doers as to the deeds. Men of virtue, not the definition of virtue, are the substitute "theory." There is no way to judge abstractly between a great compromiser and a crusader. We have seen how Socrates cites diverse, even opposed types as virtuous. In time the public, moreover, judges them correctly, this being implicitly the content and result of the discourse reflected in the statesmen's eudoxia. At the same time we are confronted with the public's error in assessing Anytos. This error makes the point we wish to emphasize. Anytos' claim and his desire to believe that virtue is teachable rationalize orthodoxy and the resort to labels and clichés as the content of it. So long as he can keep speech and discourse at this level, there is no adequate judgment of him or other leaders. Public opinion could not have the time-tested character which Socrates sets up as the condition of evaluation. There may then be a society of consent in name, but not in fact. Apart from reasonably adequate discourse, a bare vote is often mere unreliable consent.

Besides the traits we have discussed the discourse would have other features in the process of decision-making, but we consider these in chapters 7 and 9 in discussing the theory of action and method. Our purpose here is only to set the background for the problem of the acquisition of virtue. We merely generalize the discourse of Socrates with Anytos and Meno in which he reads off from the deeds of the leaders of Athens a rule attachable to them and applicable in turn to the particular problem of the repressive tendencies of Anytos. The discourse provides the methods and models, and occasions for engagement, by means of which youths open to the inspiration needed for future guidance can undergo a kind of learning like that envisaged by Theognis. For society's sake alone, however, this "learning" cannot be passive; it must involve the participation of the young in the processes of the discourse. Discovery of the talent within themselves does not lie simply in appreciation of what has been done, but in their own discourse directed to present problems. Society can discover them only there also; the discourse must be read rightly of course, but the stakes are incalculable.

We have described something like exemplary discourse for the political problem and spoken of the young as involved in it. But this is an open society, and even the appearance and effectiveness of the exemplary discourse as we described it is not possible if there is some antecedently fixed requirement for it. Such a requirement then becomes itself a rigid orthodoxy. The youth must also cut their teeth on, as the society must entertain, diversity of utopian theories, isms, and so forth. There is risk in this, as we have said before, but there is reason to hope, if occasion warrants, that the primacy of achievements as the relevant "theory" and of the maintenance of the state as the result will win out. The politics of *eudoxic* guidance claims that the openness it posits and sees as essential to the achievements that have been made, is the best chance for civilized men to minimize the risks. To put this less grandly, this openness offers the best chance of bringing the finest youths to the point of discovering and giving effect to the right opinions in the particular circumstances, for openness carries with it a recognition of the magnitude of the object being dealt with and its resistance to final formulations.

We end our account of the political theory in the *Meno* by emphasizing its stress not on theoretical principles of social structure or whatever, but on the actually existing state. This must work within the limitations incident to its existential character and its possession of resources within these limits needed for attaining both freedom and continuity. The search in the dialogue has been not for fixed principles but rather for the operations most likely to produce a Meno or an Anytos as well as a Pericles or even a Socrates. The resultant operations are of a sort, however, which are probably open only for a philosopher with an idealistic appreciation of the role and nature of principles.

We believe that in that respect also, Plato's feat in writing the *Meno* is a remarkable one. We have at times gone beyond the letter of the dialogue, but we have done this having in mind our own close analysis of the text (87B–100C) in chapter 5. The present chapter must also accord with the final results of the dialogue on the epistemological issues implied in the operational political approach. We pass in chapter 7 to these results.

7 Knowing and Opining

Particular Facts

The incompatibility between the result of the hypothetical argument ("virtue is teachable") and that of the Anytos episode ("virtue is not teachable") provides the conditions for the final argument of the *poion* section (pt. III) and of the dialogue as a whole. The conditions are 1) the turning "of our minds" from external sources (Gorgias and Prodicus as guides for Meno and Socrates respectively) to "ourselves" (96E), and 2) the combining of "virtue is useful" from the hypothetical argument with the emphasis on "useful men" from the Anytos episode to yield "good men are useful" as the principle of the final argument (97A).

As we have noted, the "turning of our minds on ourselves" is not a return to a slave-boy inquiry into recollection, but, rather, a reflection upon Meno and Socrates as good men concerned with the values in their societies. In turning on himself and his companion, Socrates remakes his basic distinction between knowledge and opinion, and then Meno responds to the inherent values of opinion. This is brought out clearly by three theses not commonly found in Plato, which emerge. We shall use them as topics for developing the significance of this argument and extending it into a new Platonic conception of action. The three are: (i) There is knowledge of particular fact. (ii) The consequences of knowledge and right opinion are identical. (iii) Virtue is right opinion and not knowledge.

(i)   Knowing Particulars

On occasion, Plato treats factual particulars as imitations of ideas (forms). The forms are universals in which particulars participate. The well-recognized two-world theory based on the proportion, being is to becoming as knowledge is to opinion (*Phaedo*—78 ff, *Republic*—510), clearly reduces or even dissolves factual particulars into a particular combination of metaphysically more fundamental entities, the Forms.

The argument of the *Meno*, however, is designed along quite different lines—lines which give significance to our knowledge of fact. Such knowledge is not reducible to a concatenation of known universal forms. The preparation for this is indicated by points made earlier. First, the original subject is man's acquisition of virtue as a good external to himself. Second, this acquisition is made to depend upon knowing the object in the same way that one knows Meno, by being acquainted with him.[1] Third, conceptual particulars are knowable, as illustrated by the slave-boy episode.

Further, the determination of particular fact as knowable is not designed as a purely theoretical exercise; rather, it is an essential step in an inquiry into the foundations of human action, and in particular, into the notion of virtue as possessed by men as a guide for their actions. In pursuing this goal, Plato clarifies the distinction between "knowing particular facts" and "opining particular facts." The man who has traveled from Athens to Larisa *knows* the way; the man who is told or reads a road map merely opines this fact.

We indicated in chapter 3 that Plato applies his notion of knowing concepts (slave-boy knowledge) to our knowing particular facts. The principal domain of knowledge is indeed the conceptual, and this provides the analogue for our knowing particulars. The analogy consists of the identification of the extremes and the link between them in each case: a square and its double linked by the framework, diagonal, and isosceles right triangles in the slave-boy instance and Athens and Larisa linked by the road between them as directly experienced. (We leave to chap. 8 the question of the tripartite structure of causes operative in experience.)

What is immediately experienced is a known fact, a whole with ordered parts. Plato denies here that knowledge is always right and true opinion is sometimes wrong, because true opinion is *never* wrong (97C–D). He argues instead that knowledge is more stable, longer lasting; yet his argument rests ultimately upon the earlier one to the effect that learning is recollection, in which opinions are "made fast with causal reasoning"—thereby turning into knowledge and becoming more permanent. This reversion to the double-square problem in order to make this distinction, in a context in which Plato demonstrates not absolute eternality of knowledge but merely longer duration, indicates the factual bearings of the distinction between knowledge and true opinion. The causal connection in the particular known facts is just the middle between extremes, as is, for example, the road from Athens to Larisa as experienced.

It may be objected that this middle has no mathematically necessary connection between the two extremes such as the causal connectors have in the double-square problem. True enough; but now the extremes are not geometric entities either. It is also true that if one starts at Socrates' Athens and follows a given path, one arrives at Meno's Larisa. It is wrong to seek mathematical necessity in a succession of physical events taken separately, though one can of course reason analogically from the total pattern of extremes and middle in the geometrical case to a total pattern experienced in the other.

To insist upon mathematically necessary connectors is to reduce the factual particular to a sum of a vast number of universal relationships that any such particular imitates or participates in; for example, all the necessary relationships of physics, astronomy, chemistry, geology, geography, biology, psychology, sociology, which placed Athens, Larisa, and the path between them where they are, and which produced Socrates and Meno respectively as identifiable citizens in each city-state. In this process of reduction, one never *knows* a particular fact but can only have opinions about it.

It might be objected that characterizing knowledge as longer-lasting than true opinion by reference to the causal reasoning or recollection in the slave-boy episode cuts short any attempt to apply this to knowledge of particular facts. Yet Plato's attention to the temporal realm and his neglect of reference to an eternal (as found, for instance, in the *Phaedo*'s but not the *Meno*'s conception of the immortality of the soul) appear to justify applying this notion to experienced or known fact. What can it mean, though, to say that knowledge about a fact is more stable than an opinion about it? It does not mean either of the extreme possibilities one could abstractly conceive—either that an opinion based only on the words of another lacks any existential reference, or that knowledge of a fact as experienced is indestructible, no matter how fragile the object experienced and no matter how fallible our memory of the experience. The opinion is a genuine cognition, and the factual knowledge is subject to contingency! To say factual knowledge is not so subject would place temporal events in an atemporal context, like Spinoza's modes. Instead the view that knowledge of particular fact is more stable than opinion remains a matter of commonsense experience; what we experience directly makes a longer-lasting impression on our minds than what we are merely told or gather from a map. This knowledge lasts as long as our memory is unimpaired and physical conditions remain as they are between Athens and Larisa.

This connection of knowledge with memory at the factual level is no mere chance. Recollection of what has been directly experienced does last much longer than recollection of what we merely have been told. This is especially true when we are seeking for connecting links between extremes in a particular whole fact, that is, for causal reasoning about such particulars. The dialogue can be read as developing in terms of various concepts of memory, from the memory that Meno retains of Gorgias' teachings, through the recollection of the slave-boy, to the factual memory involved in knowledge of particulars. The work can also be viewed as going from a memory of relatively empty words whose significance was not clear even when accepted as important by Meno, through a basic identity of the human mind with all that is conceptually available to it by means of inquiry, to the experiential memories available to each man.

We turn to our own last question: Why does Plato introduce this distinction between knowledge and opinion at this factual level when his interest is in consequences of action where the differences between knowledge and opinion disappear? Knowledge of particulars is available to all men individually and is sharable by one man through words which convey to others similar concepts—though these are only opinions. One cannot move from these opinions through words back to the originals of knowledge (as experienced) from which they arose and this contrasts sharply with the movement of the slave-boy by questioning from opinions toward knowledge in discovering conceptual particulars. This dialogue is concerned with particular actions in the *temporal flow* in which knowledge neither of conceptual particulars (e.g., the double square) nor of factual particulars may be possible. The only solid foundation, however, for a cognitive structure dealing with actions in a temporal flow is direct acquaintance. This provides the content from which any judgments about the appropriate acts and probable outcomes may be formulated. There is indeed a use being made of the past and of our knowledge, by memory, of past facts. Though not determining the right action this at least provides the materials on which right opinion depends in making a judgment even about novel situations. For this reason, the fundamental Platonic thesis that knowledge is sharply distinct from opinion even within a temporal context must still be maintained when the argument narrows to the problem of action and its consequences.

(ii)   *Identity of Actional Consequences of*
           Knowledge and Right Opinion

We note several points relating to the practical consequences of knowledge and right opinion. First, knowledge and opinion are not being identified; Socrates maintains steadfastly that this distinction is "not at all a conjecture with me but something I would particularly assert that I knew" (98B). This point is explored in section iv below. Second, the words translated as "knowledge" in this argument are both *phronēsis* and *epistēmē*, with the former apparently indicating the prudential aspect, the latter, the self-constituted structure. *Sophia* (wisdom and the cognate, wise) and *nous* (mind or reason) are linked with *epistēmē*, for the great politicians are not really wise (*sophia*). That is, they have no ultimate paradigm of knowledge, nor do they possess mind (*nous*), the ordered disposition of knowing. Third, the opinion is true (*alethēs*) when it corresponds to the facts; it is right (*orthē*) as a guiding principle in action. Fourth, the central concept is that of a good man who acts rightly, that is, attains useful consequences in action whether this be based upon knowledge or opinion. The principle of a good man is not wisdom but good opinion (eudoxia), a more specific notion of right and true opinion which conveys the idea of right action and good repute.

Because one cannot possibly experience a particular future fact, and because one's knowledge of any fact arises in a completed direct experience, we cannot know a future fact though we may have right opinion about it. We may ask, then, what it means to say that the actional consequences of knowledge and of right opinion are identical, when knowledge of the future consequences is impossible?

This question however, has already been answered. Knowledge of particular facts is memory; a man who has gone from Athens to Larisa acts upon that knowledge when he makes the journey again, yet the outcome may be the same as it is for a man who has never made the trip previously but who has a good map. Nevertheless, the state of mind of the two men is not identical despite the identity of the consequences. The greater stability of the impressions of a man possessing knowledge involves a whole contextual structure. If, for example, a landmark identified on the map or described to the inexperienced traveler has been destroyed, he will undoubtedly become lost, for a time at any rate, but the experienced traveler soon sees the predicament and orients himself again, using less prominent features of the terrain. For the map reader, of course, either right opinion is missing or else a wrong opinion (that a landmark is available) takes its place, so this case is no counter-example to the general proposition that right opinion is as useful as knowledge in guiding our actions.

But even for the man who knows a particular fact, that is, who has had a complete experience of the road, one cannot say he knows a *future* fact. For on a given day a man in Athens, intending to go to Larisa, cannot claim to know that he will be in Larisa the next day. He may be prevented or at least delayed. Knowledge of future facts is impossible. Thus, in a projection of our knowledge of a past fact to achieve a given consequence (a new fact), knowledge and right opinion are useful in different ways. No historical dialectic such as Hegel's, based as it is on some concrete reality underlying fact, is sufficient to overcome the existential indeterminacy that inheres in action.

Right opinion cannot provide causal reasoning; that is, the connecting link between the idea envisaged as the outcome of the action and the actual termination of the action. If this is out of the question for an Athenian intending to go to Larisa, it is clearly all the more impossible for a person in high political office to know that he can achieve an intended end, though much experience and keen sensitivity to all available elements in a total situation will more likely lead to right actions. Thus using as the standard the causally structured acquaintance knowledge of the mind in its conceptual knowing, Socrates has shown what it means to know particular facts and has also shown the sense in which right opinion is as good as knowledge in serving as a guide for action. It provides the same consequences which knowledge would have provided had the causal connections constituting knowledge been available.

(iii)   *Virtue is Good Opinion* (Eudoxia)

We have noted the incompatibility of the fact that there are no teachers of virtue with the normal Socratic maxim, "Virtue is knowledge." As a fitting alternative notion—not a definition—of virtue as it is found in everyday life, Socrates suggests that it is right opinion. Since right opinion yields as useful a consequence as does knowledge, and since knowledge alone links conditions and consequences causally (opinion lacks this causal necessity, either conceptual or physical), we must discover what it means to say that opinion is right.

We return to Socrates' third model definition (76A–D) which Meno found so satisfactory and which appears to us to be a clue to this question. Color was defined through the commensurateness of the moving parts (effluences) to the opening of the eye; that is, the fit of each of these to the other. This definition contrasts sharply with the suggested explanatory grounds (harmonies) for sight and hearing in the *Republic* VII, however sketchy the suggestions found there may be. This Empedoclean-Gorgian definition of color served as a model for the third definition of virtue, which turned on the fittingness of the goods acquired for the person acquiring them. It failed because saying that a fit was required involved saying that the acquiring of goods was accomplished in accord with a part of virtue—namely, justice. Thus, the definition lacked the causal reasoning necessary to connect the agent with the object acquired and for this reason it was not properly constituted knowledge.

In both definitions the notion of fittingness applies to parts in relation to each other within a total system. Socrates finds neither of them to be a conceptually adequate definition. The remainder of the dialogue is designed to achieve the mode of cognition which is appropriate to (*fits*) the question originally raised: "how virtue comes to man." Right opinion is that cognitive state which guides our action to a successful consequence—that which knowledge (with its causal connections) would have produced had it been available. Right opinion is not merely true; does not merely use words corresponding to facts, but directly uses words as guides to action in order to affect new facts. Thus, the notion of a *fit* between ideas and facts, where causal links are unavailable, is the basic ingredient of right opinion.

Human excellence in leadership is the basic source of good for all men, despite the absence of a causal connection between man and his possession of virtue by which virtue might be systematically transmitted from one man to another. The lack of such a causal connection implies that men of right opinion do act without comprehension, or sense, or understanding. Thus, good opinion (eudoxia) is not a common characteristic of the human mind, available to all men as is the conceptual knowledge elicited from the slave-boy. This point is supported by witnesses notoriously without concepts in the Greek world: Spartans and women! They give verbal support that the few men of excellence are divinely inspired and that good opinion is a divine gift (99D).

Such divine dispensation is not needed in *Republic* VI, where the inquiry reaches the most central doctrines about human knowledge. Where causal connections are missing, however, such a godlike agency *is* required. This is Plato's deus ex machina supplied where a causal account is not available. In fact, the appeal to the gods indicates that for Plato the argument is cognitively limited. (A comparison with the Augustinian notion of belief as superior and basic to knowledge comes to mind.)

(iv)   *The* Meno's *Theory of Action*

Now we treat an application of Plato's distinction between knowledge and opinion in a context of a particular fact or action, in order to clarify the relation of the cognitive elements intrinsic to the action. Though Plato here as elsewhere centers his analysis on the concept of virtue, the *Meno* also provides a view of the existential problems of action quite close to many modern theories. Actions are cognitively informed in the *Meno*, not mere mechanical or physiological motions. In routine situations the cognitive element may merge with the acquired habit of action and become a generalized knowledge or art which can be reapplied on subsequent occasions even as the assurance of the outcome is more firmly established. We customarily respond in many cases, for example, in running from danger. Though a machine can be devised which would respond similarly to specified dangers (heat and smoke), this merely shows that we can construct mechanisms with automatic triggering devices and capabilities for movement that are similar to responses which we have had to acquire through experience and habituation.

We also know from experience that other persons act as we do, since our own actions support, interlock with, or oppose those of others. Even if a Daedalus or a Turing could construct a machine which could function like a man, we might confuse its motions with human actions on a given occasion only if we were not sufficiently aware of its construction and mode of operation.

When we consider actions which we have neither participated in nor observed, but learned about from the words of others, our cognition is merely an opinion. Most cognitions of historical particulars and of generalizations of empirical facts are what Russell called knowledge by description and what Plato treats as descriptive opinion. Only those who act can know the causal connection which the action performed has borne to the two extremes of circumstances and consequences, and they can know only retrospectively. It follows, then, that the two statements "Virtue is right opinion" and "Virtue is a gift of the gods" are both opinions. Each goes far beyond any particular action and its completion.

We see also the centrality of cognition as informing every action if we consider the limits of action—and this in two contrary directions. First, contemporary action theory has raised the question of just what the action is. For example, in a killing, is the act a defense of a man's house, the contraction of the muscles in his finger, or the motion of the neurons in the brain? An affirmative answer to the last possibility places the muscle contraction among the *consequences* of the action. From the point of view of the *Meno*, the answer is clear. The "lower" limit of the action is determined by the scope of the opinion informing the action. Clearly, no agent opines about brains neurons, or about muscle contraction; untutored persons may opine about the way to squeeze a trigger, but more experienced men defend a house against an intruder, and scarcely consider how they will handle a pistol. The opinion thus sets the "lower" limits, even in cases where the opinion is incorrect. Thus, if the intruder is the homeowner's son who has lost his key and does not wish to awaken his parents to be let in, the shooting is not really a defense of the house, in spite of what the owner may be thinking as he pulls the trigger.

Second, the ancients asked the larger question of the limits of an action—the "upper" limits. For example, Aristotle inquires about an action relative to a whole life (social, not merely biological) in which the chief good is happiness. Herodotus traces the completing of an action through five generations from Gyges to Croesus in explaining Croesus' defeat by Cyrus as a consequence of Gyges' killing of his king, Candaules, at the instigation of Candaules' wife. The theory of action in the *Meno* is problematic in sharp contrast to Herodotus' comprehensive account of action; that is, it has an "upper" limit set by the opinion of the agent which informs the action—even in those cases where the opinion is incorrect.

The "upper" limit is not a fixed time period, but is determined by the scope of the action envisaged. Thus the duration varies from the fraction of a second spent shooting an intruder to the months Columbus spent sailing to the West Indies. Of more significance is the fact that the consequences of most actions proliferate beyond those envisaged by the agents themselves—even if the intruder was in fact a robber and the Indies were what Columbus anticipated. Nevertheless, the opinion informing the action roughly determines its temporal limits, the envisaged proximate consequences of the action (including geographic discoveries) as distinct from the proliferating of more distant ones (founding new nations), and the ultimate success or failure of the action.

Columbus' sailing westward to find new trade routes to the Indies provides us with an example not only of an action as a temporally extended event, but also of one whose aims are only partially defined. He was unsuccessful in a narrow sense, having found no route for East Indian trade, but was successful in the larger sense, as having opened up a new world (as a proximate consequence) and therewith a projection into hitherto unknown possibilities. The act as guided by opinion thus gets its determinacy from the unexpected results achieved and in the larger sense the opinion guiding the action has been right, since it would have been done had men known of the possibilities. Many scientific discoveries are of this sort.

In this account of action as cognitively informed we have used both the terms, *opinion* and *knowledge*, yet in the *Meno* Socrates maintains the fundamental Socratic principle that knowledge is distinct from opinion. This distinction as it bears on our view of a particular action entails a two-stage view—prospective and retrospective—about action and the role of cognition as causative. First, in advance of an action, one's prospective cognitions—for example, taking stock, planning, rehearsing, holding an end in view—are opinions which parallel the circumstances-action-consequences of overt activity. Such a prospective parallel is not causal, being merely a guide to an outcome not assured, to an action not yet completed. The consequence pictured may not occur as anticipated. Second, after the action, one retrospectively grasps the total experience serially as a causal nexus in which the cognitive element (knowledge) is firmly attached to the action and its consequences. One then knows whether the action was successful or not and whether the opinion which guided it was right or wrong. This double view, of parallel-prospective and serial-retrospective, provides a flexible theory of action. In chapter 9, we shall develop the implications further in a brief discussion of the relation between thought and action and of the freedom-determinism controversy.

The slave-boy episode, with its conceptual discoveries of causal links, is thus supplemented by a theory of human action based on opinions when knowledge is not available until the action is completed. This leaves Socrates dissatisfied—he has to depart at the end. This evidential approach differs from the conceptual structures of other dialogues, and apparently, in leaving Socrates dissatisfied, also leaves unopened the conceptual possibilities of the chief terms; for example, *virtue*. That Plato's methods allow for a development toward this operational solution shows the flexibility of his idealism.

(v)   *Gods as the Source of Virtue in Man*

Having argued that virtue is right opinion rather than knowledge because it is not teachable, Socrates maintains that human excellence, as found in political leaders such as Themistocles, Aristides, and Pericles, is divinely inspired. Men whose opinions fitted the facts and yielded successful outcomes had good reputations as political leaders and they also had good opinions as relatively stable bases for guiding the state. The very regularity of such opinions indicates that they cannot be a matter of mere chance. Hence the men were called divine or godlike because they "succeed in many a great deed and word." They are classed with other divinely inspired persons who do not know whereof they speak (99C).

Clearly, political leaders do not know, even as they successfully and repeatedly decide how to act under given circumstances, exactly how they must secure the best possible outcome. Tracing the source of good opinion to the gods is simply recognizing the cognitive limits of any human account for such extraordinary talents. This account of the source of good opinion constitutes not knowledge but merely true opinion. As such, it is not directly provable, but is a result of the approximative technique used in the dialogue to get solutions to questions which cannot be answered by pure conceptual analysis.

The limits of the argument are shown not merely in the conclusion that virtue is divinely inspired, but also in the determination of the unachieved ideal of a statesman who could make another man into a statesman. The only example of this that Socrates gives is from Homer's account of Teiresias who alone "has his mind" (100A). In Hades the time-dimension is meaningless, so Teresias' knowledge is no guide. His advice to statesmen in this world is unheeded or is offered too late (*Oedipus Rex, Antigone*); and Odysseus must journey to Hades to get it.

The closest approximation to such an ideal in this world is clearly Socrates himself, who in the *Meno* (as in many other dialogues) can be understood as a teacher of virtue—including political virtue. We indicated in chapter 1 that Socrates could function as a teacher much as the poet Theognis suggests (95D–E). Yet he disclaims having any such knowledge or making any such effort. Moreover, he fails by those same consequential standards which he has applied to other statesmen. Socrates can claim only to discover and perhaps help prepare a person whom the gods may choose to inspire. Certainly, his penultimate remark, that we must turn from asking about the acquisition of virtue to a question about its nature, reinforces the limits one reaches in pursuing this evidential question. And his last remark, when he sends Meno to persuade Anytos about Meno's newly acquired beliefs, indicates what he (as a statesman) apparently has hoped to achieve for Athens in undertaking this *poion* inquiry.

Part Three: Conclusions and Extensions

8 Forms of Discourse, Approximative Method and Operational Structure

Most passing comments, as we said earlier in this book, from Aristotle[1] onward have concentrated on the first two sections of the *Meno*, those sections on definition and geometrical search, to the neglect of the chief arguments in the *poion* section. For our part, we have argued that the first two sections are not merely attempts to define an essence (of virtue) or to recollect pure geometric knowledge, but that they are steps toward solving a practical problem, they are a preparation for overt action. In chapter 1, we argued the dramatic unity of that preparation. The last sign that something has really been achieved is that Socrates himself breaks off the colloquy. Although he speaks of the need for a definition, Socrates invites no further inquiry but must be on his own way (100B). A reason for this is that in the *Meno* a conclusion *is* reached, albeit a limited one, and Socrates' departure coincides with his effort to put that conclusion to use through Meno. Socrates exposes no flaw in the argument which leads to this conclusion. The statement that virtue is a gift of the gods, is only right opinion, not knowledge. This is why Socrates does not claim that it is a clear one. Nonetheless, he shows Meno the respect in which right opinion is as good as knowledge (97C), that is, for purposes of action. Socrates would hardly emphasize this if his purpose were to discredit it. Furthermore, his remark pertains to action, not theory, when he says that Meno will do Athens a service if he goes to Anytos and persuades him of what he, Meno, has just been persuaded.

These observations on the dialogue's practical outcome provide a point of reference for the actional, operationist interpretation which we have been following from the beginning. In this chapter we shall, to some extent, expand this interpretation; but mainly we propose to show how it gives continuity to the argument in three ways: (i) in the forms of discourse; (ii) in the bracketing structure or approximative technique which provides the general, consistently used method of the argument; and (iii) in the special form which the dialogue's idealist framework of methods takes because it is centered upon opinion-guided action.

(i)   Forms of Discourse

We differentiate the forms of discourse as the dialogue moves forward primarily in terms of the roles of the speakers involved in each exchange. The primary point is that the forms used in the sections on definition and recollection respectively provide models for the final *poion* section. This relation is immediately evident in the analogy between the initial laying down of definitions and the subsequent laying down of hypotheses in the *poion* section; and a second analogy between the inquiry in the passage on recollection and the subsequent search for a teacher of virtue in the Anytos episode. The final argument—the one coming after the proof that there are no teachers of virtue in the Anytos episode (96E–100C—see chap. 7)—apparently has no place in this simple schema; we will deal with this later. In general, we find the operationist cast in all these forms pervasive, though in different ways for different forms. While the definitional section is purely cognitive, its function of modeling and preparing for the hypothetical section helps explain why it ends with a concern for the acquisition of objects. Similarly, the slave-boy episode, while purely conceptual, relies heavily on visible evidence and concludes by stimulating Socrates to commitment on action; both of these features foreshadow the Anytos episode's search for empirical facts and Socrates' adherence to his conclusions regardless of the threats of Anytos. The relation between these models and the things modeled on them is not that of a pure or absolute form to some imperfect approximation or imitation of it, nor that of a pure theory to an application of it. Rather, that which is modeled, the analogue, has its own specific and peculiar objective within its area of operation; it uses the model for its own purposes; and it is not merely some lesser variant of the model. Further, since the *poion* objectives are primary for the dialogue, the prior theoretic models are adjusted to serve them. Structurally the models are theoretically less than wholly "pure." We now proceed serially through the modes of discourse, attending to the special role of each within the general governing relations just sketched, and culminating in the final section to which the whole points. (A summary chart of these forms is presented in Appendix, sec. ii).

Theoretic Models. The sections on definition and recollection are respectively *eidetic* (71D, 72C) and *heuristic* (86C). The eidetic problem is to win acceptance for a proposition which is already known to the master and which he presents or "tells" (*eipein*—70A, 71D). The heuristic problem is one of making a discovery in an unknown region, and proceeds by questioning (*erotein*—82E), even if tendentious. The principal part of the heuristic process is *zētetic* (inquiring—81E), which is set against *didactic* (82A, 82E), particularly insofar as this does not proceed by questioning or depend on recognition of a truth once hit upon. Both the eidetic and the zetetic aim at cognitive results, but the differences in the roles of the participants and their purposes are so great as to make extreme variants. At the eidetic extreme Gorgias purports to know everything men could want to know; at the other, strictly speaking, the slave-boy knows nothing of the subject except the language in which it is couched. Eidetic proceeds here by an abrupt presentation of supposed truths, and would lend itself to a random exhibition of existent knowledge rather than a structuring of it; and zetetic here stays within the limits of the slave-boy's very untutored sense of the terms "square," "equal," and so on. Although the two methods are intellectual by contrast with those of part III, yet these features give them an operationist cast. Let us examine both of them in detail.

In the eidetic method there are three possible ways of proceeding (corresponding respectively to the three model definitions): eristic (75C), dialectical (75D), and poetic (76E). These models are differentiated by the relations which the participants have to each other and to the proposition under dispute or other considerations. In eristic the participants are antagonists, and the proposition should be a defensible truth without regard to whether the opponent understands the terms. Even an objection from him that a proffered definition has in it an undefined term (e.g., "color," when figure is defined as what follows color) would be countered by a statement that the proposition is true and that the opponent has the burden of refuting it. If the opponent is to do so he must establish a communicative bridge across which to attack. The Socratic method here seeks to preserve a truth in a situation so hostile that truth itself could not possibly be the end. (The opponent's demand for a definition of color shows his unwillingness to accept "color" as referring to the sensation.) The participants in dialectic, on the other hand, are friends, and they proceed from points acknowledged by both parties. This is how Socrates establishes the second definition of figure. Theoretically, of course, this could provide the basis for further geometrical development, but it is not so used here because of Meno's relative lack of interest in it. What appeals to him as being closest to Gorgias' technique is a poetic definition (76B–C, 79B), which of course has its own distinctive features. As eristic and dialectic involve opposed and common meanings respectively, poetic invents a system of interacting entities to account for the occurrence of an accepted phenomenon. Thus Empedocles[2] devised a system of elements to account plausibly for color (Socrates' third model definition) and Meno borrowed from Simonides a definition of virtue in terms of the power to procure goods.

This schema of opposed, common, and invented starting points, and of steadfast, fertile, and explanatory propositions, is notable also for what is absent from it. Compare the conception of dialectic here with that in the *Phaedrus*, where the dialectician must be the master of the processes of division and compounding, of conceiving the subject so organically that it can be cut at the joints, and of appraising situations and persons with a cosmological reference in mind; or with that in the *Republic*, in which dialectic must be delayed until completion of a full mathematical education. In the *Meno* the dialectician seeks in ordinary language for terms which will aid him in clarifying the definition he wishes to convey. We have outlined in chapter 2 the criteria applied to these definitions which require their cognitive integrity, especially in the case of the dialectically established definition, but these criteria apply to the internal integrity of the knowledge, not to a comprehensive base; and men communicate them in order to win them a place in the minds of other men. As we said earlier, this nontechnical treatment constitutes the operational cast of eidetic and makes it suitable to model a less rigorous method for *poion* problems, as we will see when we come to the argument by hypothesis.

The discourse with the slave-boy takes place on two levels—first-intentionally in itself and second-intentionally in the talk about it between Meno and Socrates. The discourse has three successive forms. The first, the introductory exchange between Meno and Socrates, is a poetic development of an attitude; a priestly myth is employed to ground the argument which warrants confidence or trust (*pistis*—81E) in inquiry as based on the kinship of all things. Second, relative to this pistic introduction, the zetetic exchange is a demonstration or showing (*epideixein*—82B), as we noted in chapter 3, and the questioning of the boy is accordingly ostensive—the diagram which Socrates evidently draws on the ground being an essential part of it. Third, after the showing the reflection by Meno and Socrates culminates in the expression by Socrates of a commitment to inquiry. All three forms—the trust, the showing, and the reflection—depend on exercising the zetetic method proper in the exchange with the slave-boy, enhancing its significance and strengthening conviction in its intellectual adequacy. The whole constitutes the heuristic form.

The interrogation of the slave-boy is conceptual in its interest and emphasis. Yet the relevance of ordinary opinions is great here too, for the outcome as well as the beginning is built around the boy's commonsense notions. The inquiry is geometrical, yet the geometrical principles which underlie it are unknown to the boy. The argument gets its cogency for him by isolating a causal element within the structure it builds up from his gross sense of "square" and related terms, and from the "evidence" provided by the drawings rather than by refining these diagrams and gross concepts into technically precise presuppositions.

Poion Counterparts. When the problem shifts back to the way virtue is acquired, Socrates does not treat the models as extremes and seek a form now that falls between them, that is, between *dicta* being presented by the master, on the one hand and, on the other, ideas growing from within the respondent. Instead of seeking this middle immediately, Socrates moves toward it in stages by adapting or slightly modifying each of the models in turn. His own stance shifts also as he moves into the role of a guide, distinct from that of the authoritarian master, and also from that of the mere stimulator of ideas. The general form of discourse here, coordinate with the eidetic and heuristic, is *doxic*.

The early part of the dialogue provides the models here, but they are being tested for their value in coping with the problems at hand, and are modified accordingly. In the hypothetical-didactic argument which we examined in chapter 4, Socrates sets up a proposition: Knowledge alone is teachable, presented and maintained like any of the model definitions in the section on definitions. The critical difference, however, is that the proposition is not presented for its own sake. In the problem of whether the triangle is inscribable and whether virtue is teachable the basic proposition is rather presented strictly for instrumental purposes, that is, for its use in constructing a syllogism to work out the problem of inscribing a triangle or determining the teachability of virtue. The hypothesis is "plain to everyone," and as discursively followed up is then referred to by Plato as *ex hypotheseōs skeptesthai*—inspecting the question at issue.

The roles of the participants shift also. Although Socrates lays down here the basic hypothesis that knowledge alone is teachable as positively as he presented definitions in the eidetic section, he now sets out from it on a course of reasoning intended clearly to take Meno along with him. That he does so is evident from Meno's being the one who draws the conclusion from the syllogism that Socrates builds up and in his being loath to yield to Socrates' statement of doubt about the validity of the conclusion. For a technical term here the language cited above would suggest the label "hypothetico-scopic" since this suggests Socrates' leading role and Meno's participation.

No doubt this form lacks self-sufficiency for practical reasoning, and for getting a bearing on the situation, or question, with which the speakers are concerned. The next shift (the Anytos episode) is accordingly set up as a check on the preceding hypothetical method, since the latter cannot be definitive with regard to particulars. This new discourse is a search modeled on the slave-boy inquiry—but this is a joint search (*syzētetic*—90B) in which the participants search for facts and prove their findings. Socrates' role as guide in this case is more pronounced, however; he marks out which kinds of facts are relevant to the search for the existence of teachers, the success or failure of claimants, and the determination of public opinion. It is still of course up to the respondent to see the significance of the facts thus marked out. Anytos balks, but Meno concurs, suggesting that a necessary feature of this form of discourse, concerned with value though it may be, is the bearing it has on the fortunes or cherished opinions of the participants. Obviously, however, the participants must also have experience with the facts; hence Anytos is a necessary type of participant. Meno is better because he is not threatened by the facts, but for that very reason the facts he knows are less important than the ones Anytos knows. Nonetheless, since the import of the facts in both Thessaly and Athens is the same, the syzetetic form of discourse is sharply distinguished from the hypothetical.

Culminating Poion Form. This opposition is reconciled in the method of the final part of the dialogue—persuasive reasoning (*peithein logismōi*—100B). It is distinct from causal reasoning (*aitias logismōi*—98A), and as a sort of doxic guidance it proceeds in a novel way. It is not a simple adaptation of either of the two preceding practical forms, but it reconciles the originally incompatible hypothetical and syzetetic forms.

The participants have no simple master-disciple relation. Socrates is perplexed. His perplexity is not a literary device, but a real difficulty in the belief he has professed. He must receive the inspiration—that will resolve the problem. But in view of Meno's limited abilities, this inspired insight cannot be an overarching concept; it must in fact still be in accord with Meno's chief opinions. The inspiration begins with making the distinction between knowledge and opinion turn on their relative duration, their effectiveness. By drawing the distinction here, Socrates can fill out the inspiration by maintaining the unequivocal rightness of right opinion. This of course is the novel element although it is in a sense a tautology. What is the meaning and basis of the novelty? To say that an opinion is right means that nominally it applies to the immediate case at hand. But we know that it might not apply to the next case; and in our normal way of judging that an opinion would now apply but another time would not apply, we arrive at the common notion of opinion as being sometimes right and sometimes wrong. Socrates' tautological statement that right opinion is always right has to mean that it is itself inseparable from the immediate case at hand to which it does apply. Grasping the opinion as right is grasping it as giving a meaning to the situation as in fact determinately efficacious. It is evident therefore that in content this novel resolution that Socrates develops preserves the cognitive element for which the hypothetical argument provided the basis, and at the same time explains why virtue is not teachable. It is clearly persuasive, because it rests on opinion of opinions previously accepted but not used for or adapted to the case at hand—the acquisition of virtue.

We have already sketched in Socrates' role as the guide in this form of discourse. He has to be inspired, and inspired in a way that can appeal to and have an effect upon Meno. Inspiration obviously cannot do this by depending on Meno to draw a deductive inference as he did in the hypothetical section; nor should he be merely dazzled or bewildered as he was at the end of the Anytos episode. Between these he must feel himself, as he does, a genuine participant in the thinking, grasping its results now as a novel notion which is the resolution of the problem at hand. Its actual value underpins the acceptance of what he believes and of what provides the solution to the problem.

The Model for Persuasive Reasoning. Though neither recollection nor the eidetic form of discourse, in which the master presents the solution to the disciple, provided the answer for the final exchange; the poetic, or inventive mode of the third model definition and of the third attempt to define virtue did offer a systematic account of color and of virtue. The solution which Socrates has found also takes account of the total context of circumstances which enters into any right opinion as the basis for action on a given occasion. The actor invents, if he is inspired, what is most fitting for the circumstances. Though the heuristic form in which a conceptual discovery emerges from within the inquirer as he pursues his theoretical problem afforded no answer, the reflective mode emphasizes the implications of a successful empirical inquiry, thus providing an analogue for man's receptivity of divine inspiration in matters external to him.

These two kinds of discourse when taken together emphasize the duality of the prospective-retrospective views constituting the operation of persuasive reasoning in action. A man attuned to the movement of events (including the civic state of mind) in which he repeatedly finds the persuasive basis for leading the citizens to decisions best in the circumstances is indeed a man of virtue. (Virtue here is not an art or other form of knowledge by acquaintance.) Such a man is certainly blessed with a divine gift.

In summary, then, the forms of discourse[3] carry the dialogue from essences and cognitive structures to reasoning about action. Socrates makes this shift, thereby with poetic sanction himself becoming the paradigm of a virtuous man. That is, in his determination that virtue is right opinion and a divine gift, he affects Meno's beliefs and performs a political act, as we suggested in chapter 1. One might argue retrospectively that Socrates failed. Meno did not persuade Anytos, who brought Socrates to trial and eventually to his execution. Yet this judgment of consequences does not prove that Socrates fell short of the best that the circumstances allowed, both with Meno and with the slave-boy. It merely proves that though Meno's opinion was such that changing it slightly was a likely mode of attack upon the problem at hand, other factors in the situation were too resistant to allow either Meno to be moved to action or Anytos to be moved by Meno.

(ii)   *Method of Approximation—Bracketing*

In arguing for the tripartite structure of the dialogue in chapter 2 as well as in discussing the forms of discourse in section i above, we indicated that the basic method of the dialogue was one of approximation by what gunnery officers call bracketing. Such a method is particularly suited to problems whose solution cannot be exactly determined by direct rational procedures, for example in the closer and closer determination of the value of an irrational number by systematically under- and overshooting the actual value. Where, as in the *Meno*, the problem admits no direct rational approach, the bracketing technique is most fitting. Its specific form varies in the sections devoted to definition, to the slave-boy, and to the *poion* question. Each of the early sections illustrates and provides a sort of methodological paradigm, but clearly the choice of the method for the dialogue is a function of its worth for the *poion* section. After noting first how the slave-boy episode provides a paradigm, we will emphasize the use of the sections on definition and slave-boy respectively as the general outer brackets for the overshooting and under-shooting. Within these the special problems and resolution of the *poion* section are dealt with.

a) Though the slave-boy episode does present a solution designed for the problem posed, it exhibits the method of bracketing. The argument moves from two as the length of the side of the given square to four as the apparent double to the false middle (three). This approx-imation clearly is an incorrect solution—one which leads, as we have seen, to the correct middle (the diagonal). Plato knew that the numeri-cal value of this line could not be expressed by rational numbers, and could be approximated only by bracketing though this fact does not enter into the problem as posed.

b) Besides thus exhibiting the bracketing method within itself, the slave-boy episode as a whole forms an outer bracket, as we noted, juxtaposed with the section on definition as the opposite outer brack-et. In the latter, Meno has only mechanically remembered maxims of virtue to call on. The slave-boy episode conversely does exhibit man discovering an intelligible structure or becoming acquainted with a knowable form. The *poion* section then fittingly yields an insight midway between these poles of ignorance and knowledge: an insight having some valid content but falling short of knowledge, that is, right opinion. Within this general type of cognition the conclusion is estab-lished that virtue is right opinion.

The concern of the *poion* section with this middle region of opinion is pervasive. Its three parts, the method of argument by hypothesis, the empirical method of the Anytos episode, and the method of reasonable persuasion, are all well-suited, as we have seen, for any formulating of opinion. Similarly, the subject being investigated—the "how" of such virtue as Pericles possesses—is not treatable with certitude. And the result as appraised by Socrates (that virtue is a gift of the gods) is the answer sought, but not the final truth on the matter. In each case, a middle way is found. Bracketing is no mere chance procedure for locating knowledge, but a guided trial-and-error proc-ess.

c) Similarly, the opening sections of the dialogue, again especially the slave-boy episode, play a crucial role in bringing Meno and Soc-rates together psychologically in a focus on the *poion* region as indi-cated above; for both must undergo a change—Meno from his aver-sion to an exchange in which the master does not do all and Socrates from his aversion to an inquiry which does not begin with the ques-tion about the definition of the subject under scrutiny.

As we have seen, Meno seeks for definitions among routinely remembered formulas and resists Socrates' first two model defini-tions, pressing Socrates until the third model definition emerges (color is an effluence perceptible to sight). He likes it because, according to Socrates, "you are used to the way it is put" (76D). He cannot find an adequate definition within the realm of the familiar, and he resists efforts to take him outside that realm. In his observation of the slave-boy exchange Meno could see a reflection of his own habit, that of clinging to the familiar, in the slave-boy's efforts to find answers by a routine method. The latter failed the slave-boy as the maxims did Meno. But Meno, who up to this point had strongly doubted the value of inquiry, could now see that there was an answer illuminating to the slave-boy which lay outside the routine. With Meno's total dependence on the master he would still be distrustful of being led too far from the familiar, and this could explain his disinclination to go directly into the question of what virtue is. But the success of the inquiry nonetheless provides him with hope of acquiring illumination by a modified form of inquiry. Here we are relying on Meno's obvious liking for discourse, but this *ex post facto* analysis does fit the important psychological turn which the dialogue takes at the end of the slave-boy episode. Meno moves on to the problem of acquiring virtue, for this seems safer than that of defining virtue because it rests on views which are rhetorically commonplace. The question becomes this: How do men whom we regard as virtuous come to be as they are? This substitutes one's awareness of virtuous men for the definition of virtue. Pericles exemplifies virtue as possessed and so Meno can remain within the realm of the familiar. The answer reached, however—that virtue is a gift of the gods—surprises him with its novelty. The slave-boy episode leads him to just that inquiry from which he could begin to learn.

As for Socrates' shift when it is looked at psychologically, the section on definition showed Meno's inability to cope with the rigorous criteria of unity required of a definition; and Meno's resultant paradox constitutes for Socrates something of a challenge to the power of inquiry. His choice of a problem for the slave-boy, whose answer Meno clearly knows, is important for showing whether Meno would accept Socrates' statement of the method being used with the boy. Meno does not argue, as some commentators do, that Socrates really is the master telling the answer. He sees the difference. The fact of his seeing that difference provides a reason for Socrates to feel that, though Meno will not essay the definitional inquiry, he may be drawn into some other sort of inquiry, one into the lesser but more familiar question of the acquisition of virtue. The dialogue has now reached the point of posing a genuine philosophical problem which demands investigation as distinct from a mere laying down of answers.

d) While the use of the approximative technique thus locates the subject matter and psychologically prepares for the unusual problem to be treated in it, the more notable feature is the peculiar form and power which the technique takes on in the *poion* section. We can approach this most easily through the many notions of *aporia* which develop in the three sections of the dialogue. The constitution of perplexity in fact changes in each one. In part I the perplexity is formal: Meno cannot organize his maxims and commonplaces into a definition. In part II it is demonstrative: the boy's conjecture is falsified by the exhibited structure of the subject matter. In part III it is empirical: a loosely reasoned hypothetical judgment (since virtue is knowledge it is teachable) is upset by the fact that there is no teaching of it.

These shifts become clearer in light of the status of the specious opinions, that is, those to be refuted. As we move from part to part, the specious opinion with which each of the three commences gains in plausibility because of new evidence. In part I, Meno's first answer rests on authority; he is certain, but without any sense of why he should be. To perplex him, then, it is enough to show that his beliefs cannot be formalized. In part II, the slave-boy's first conjecture is a judgment that linear doubling will work analogously for area doubling. He is not merely remembering—he has reason to believe his conjecture is right. To refute him it is necessary to show that linear doubling cannot produce a double area. In part III, a lengthy discussion establishes the specious argument (that virtue is teachable). To refute it intellectually would therefore require an inquiry into definitions which, as we saw, is precluded. Instead, Plato shows that no one in fact teaches virtue. This fact does not of itself prove the subject matter to be unteachable; thus the argument proceeds, not by looking at the structure or content of the communication but only at the results. It discredits the supposed truth that virtue is teachable by asserting that no one uses it as a premise for action. The slave-boy was refuted by being shown, not that his conjecture was never used by anyone, but that intrinsically it could not be used. This is why the refuting of him needs but one case, while in part III, refutation depends on the number and kinds of cases. This shows more specifically the sense in which the slave-boy episode guides us as a suggestive outer limit rather than as a model that can be copied.

These differences in the kinds of perplexity and their resolutions indicate the ways in which the approximative technique is especially adapted to *poion* problems of the sort dealt with here. The *poion* problem is unlike that in part I, in which even if a resolution were possible, it would be constituted of a formula entailing directly or by systematic implication the points required. Nor is the *poion* problem like that in part II, in which an altogether new way of organizing the structure enters so that its rationale is put in a new light. In both cases there is a sense in which the resolution, when found, stands by itself and does not derive meaning from a contrast or juxtaposition with the extremes between which it falls; that is, the extremes can be dropped after the answer is found. In the *poion* problem, on the contrary, the outer brackets themselves remain integral to both the situation and the solution; the cognition introduced by the hypothetical argument and the non-teachability shown in the Anytos episode remain factors in a politics based on inspiration. So also any "middle of the road" policy keeps extremes in view. *Poion* problems are indeed isolable but are so in time more than in the discipline to which they belong. The middle being sought is one fitting the whole situation.

But only to say that the middle in the bracketing technique in the *poion* section depends for its meaning on the total situation is insufficient. The resolution, as we have seen, is neither a basis of literal entailment nor a conceptual revolution in the rationale of the structure. It provides the special ground for altering the situation as one reexamines it. Here again, we are in a region which peculiarly needs something like the approximative technique.

Another advantage of taking the extremes into account, is that by so doing the investigator is placed in what may be the only condition wherein he recognizes the significance of a possible resolution—*if* he should be inspired by it. No doubt any scientist must be immersed in his problem in order to recognize the significance of an answer when it occurs to him. Here the answer remains an ingredient of the total situation that is being discussed.

These remarks on the approximative technique stress the operational features. We may add, however, that our observations show the outright necessity for an inspiration in practical affairs, since the resolution to them is not intrinsic to the situation involved. When inspiration does come it is, more than in any of the earlier parts, an external acquisition, something conferred by an outside source.

(iii)   *Operational Structure*

We have already argued that the political theory in the *Meno* is intended to provide minimal safeguards for a society of consent against the twin dangers of anti-intellectual patriotic repression on the one hand, and of actionally ineffective sophistic intellectualism on the other. This political theory contrasts sharply with that of the ideal state of the *Republic*. In this section, we will emphasize this contrast, particularly as it appears in the opening search for a definition and in the closing theory of action in each dialogue. We shall commence, for obvious reasons, with the search for definitions, proceed to the structure of conceptual inquiry and action, and finally, the notions of choice and action.

On the Search for a Definition. The search for a definition in the first book of the *Republic* touches on three topics: the nature of justice, whether or not it is a virtue, and the advantages and disadvantages of justice. These questions open up a comprehensive *ti* inquiry (Bk. II. 358B) ushering in a dialectic that progresses from momentary shadows through physical and scientific entities to ultimate forms—these latter pointing to a final insight into the source of being and knowledge. This structure provides a foundation for reexamining and evaluating forms of states that men generate and forms of lives that they lead.

The *Meno* offers no such comprehensive structure or principle for evaluation. Its attempts at definition are not productive, and they serve no more than an aporetic purpose similar to the refutative phase of contemporary philosophy (e.g., exposing misleading expressions).[4] The search for the definition of virtue which would express man's direct acquaintance with it constitutes a principle of limits in the complex of agents acting on or for objects available for acquisition. The notion of an agent acting for an object is open and cannot be satisfactorily limited by specifying some scheme of objects as the ends controlling his actions. Grammatically, the limit seems to require an adverb, not a mere noun or verb—acquiring goods virtuously. Thus, the search is for a manner by which an agent acts for an object—the manner being pivotal to the acquisition. No definition shows a limiting method applicable to the variable, indeterminate complex of agents acquiring objects. The stress on method in the rest of the dialogue (i.e., after the search for a definition) employs two criteria: a) there are disjunctive though related methods rather than a broad dialectical frame for participating elements; and b) there is a criterion of completeness within each case as distinct from a generalized whole, such as one finds in the third definition.

Yet the search for a definition is fundamental for the dialogue, for it points up the central role of the cognitive character of *all* the methods. It both rejects unreachable kinds of knowledge and sets up the criteria for cognitions that are within immediate reach: both knowledge by acquaintance and descriptive opinion. As we have seen, these two cognitive modes have helped generate a four-part structure of methods quite like the four levels of the divided line of the *Republic*, but also diverse in its intrinsic character: slave-boy, hypothetical argument, empirical argument with Anytos, and analysis of action. This is feasible because these two cognitive modes function together in every instance.

Structure of Conceptual Inquiry and Action. First, in pursuing a conceptual problem, one starts from prospective opinion that a discovery is possible. In attaining a solution, one acquires knowledge of two kinds, the first being that the conceptual discovery is causally self-constituted in the mind of the discoverer and the second, that in solving one's problem one then has also a retrospective factual knowledge of a sequence: problem-inquiry-solution. The successful practical outcome is *not* the determinant of the conceptual truth. Thus, the conceptual discovery is intrinsically bound up with the context of action. Successful discovery requires right opinion as a guide as well as earlier acquired knowledge and skills on which to open up possibilities for new insights. Multiple acts of discovery indicate that right opinion based on the acquired knowledge can be inculcated,[5] despite the fact that the talent for discovery cannot be taught.

Second, the conceptual strand in the *Meno* operates analogically in the identification of the causal components of a completed action. In conceptual discovery, three causal factors were isolated: the constitutive element, the generative source, and the framework. In a complete experience one comes to know retrospectively the causal links between the original condition and the results of the action. The act itself is the constitutive element; the opinion, the generative source; and the social consensus, the framework determinative of the valuation of the action as good, bad, inspired, and so forth.

Theory of Action. The *Republic* lays out a comprehensive system of evaluations whereby a man who understands should be enabled to make intellectual comparisons and choose that way of life affording the greatest happiness. According to the myth of Er in Book X, however, most men choose from their limited perspectives which are usually determined by their dissatisfactions with the life they have just been leading.

In the *Meno*, on the contrary, there is no such comprehensive system of values. An action is made out to be a unique relation between past and future in which cognition is at best partial and incomplete—it is mere opinion. One acts then on the shrewdest estimate for achieving the best the circumstances allow at a given moment. As the existentialists assert, man projects himself into an unknown and essentially unknowable future. Yet the theory of action in the *Meno* emphasizes not merely man's freedom in a world of nothingness (for-itself), but a particular man's being prepared in his beliefs and sensitivity to receive inspiration in making his choice of the best that the total situation may allow—a choice vitally informed by and made partly dependent on participation in appropriate discourse. Such discourse would deal with techniques that bring him closest to the problem and the ability to recognize the significance of the choice itself—a persuasion grounded in good reasons. The best that a situation may allow may not be a personal success—*vide* Socrates himself—but *any* projection will produce a complete experience.

The *Meno* employs the methods to make the connections proper to each kind of problem viewed both prospectively and retrospectively. For this reason, we have called this philosophy of connections "paragenics," following Plato's own lead in the first sentence of the dialogue (see chap. 1). The open-endedness of the prospective view of action, taken together with the continuity of right opinions of great leaders, gave Plato hope that some men were divinely inspired. The conception of divinities is introduced not as some ultimate metaphysical guarantee of the existence and knowability of things, but as a recognition of man's limits in cognition and in action along with a realization of his need for guidance in achieving the best for continued human progress.

9 General Paragenics

In the *Meno*, as we have seen, the question of how virtue comes to man is explored relative to the distinction between knowledge and opinion. In this *ti-poion* context, knowledge is longer-lasting and consists of the acquaintance of knower with known as a properly limited, causally ordered whole. Opinion is less firmly established, and consists of a derived verbal description of entities fitted together without a causal link.

The *ti-poion* distinction of the *Meno* allows for a search for the distinctive excellences in the *poion* qualities, even while retaining the superior status of the *ti* form. This is why, though the *Meno* begins with an impulse toward the *ti* form culminating in the slave-boy episode, it ends with divine inspiration so recognized as a pure acquisition and the most excellent a man can achieve for a human community.

In the *ti* inquiry of the *Republic*, the distinction between knowledge and opinion is parallel to a distinction between what is and what is opined (*ontas* and *dokountas*—334B), and again to one between being and becoming (i.e., *to on* and a mixture of *to on* and *to mē on*—478D), and to another between what is and what appears (*onta* and *phantesmata*—599A). Or again, in the *Parmenides*, a primary distinction is that between is and seems (*estin* and *phainetai*—166C). Although, as we have said earlier, Plato does suggest such proportions as a) being is to becoming as knowledge is to opinion (*Republic* V510) and b) intelligible essences (*ousia, dianoias logismōi*) are to visible changing things (*orata, mēdepote*) as knowledge is to opinion (*Phaedo*—78); these are presented in specific contexts and for specific purposes. In most cases, they are subsequently superseded after further analysis. What is clear, however, is that any additional proportion, such as that in the Meno, c) knowledge is to opinion as acquaintance is to description, cannot be used in conjunction with the earlier proportions, as though the relationship were transitive, to produce: d) intelligible essences are to visible changing things as acquaintance is to description. For both kinds of things (*duo eidē tōn ontōn*—Phaedo 78) can be either known by acquaintance or descriptively opined. One can know the causally constituted double square and the empirical fact, and one can go beyond what is known in either case by a descriptive projection which may be substantiated in later knowledge by acquaintance. Such descriptive "going beyond" is not to some "reality" intrinsic to and supportive of that with which one is acquainted. The "going beyond" to some such "reality" is consonant with proportions of type a) and b) above. Rather, acquaintance is the ground for descriptive extensions. This implies of course that the two kinds of things in the *Meno* are not the fixed metaphysical entities of the *Phaedo*, a dialogue which is pointed to stretching our experience into a realm essentially not capable of being experienced in this life.

The obvious intransitivity in the conjunction of proportions indicates clearly the sharp differences in significance attached to the distinction between knowledge and opinion and reinforces our earlier point that Plato uses such terms as these in specified contexts for particular purposes within his dialectic of definitions (see chap. 2, sec. iv). Each such inquiry exposes various facets about what is, even as the Meno examines appearances, such as acquisitions, just as they are.

The distinction between being and becoming of the *Republic* serves as grounds for the most inclusive human values that can be formulated in any comprehensive inquiry into concepts, and the distinction between is and seems of the *Parmenides* serves to frame a logico-metaphysical inquiry into the structure required for the being and intelligibility of the one and many. The distinction between acquaintance and description in the Meno is oriented to the identity of subject and object in an acquisitive relation, and it provides for an evidential inquiry concentrated upon isolable particulars.

While the former inquiries may be conceptually more fundamental for Plato, their very generality precludes their attaining an adequate grasp of existential particulars. This suggests that the ideal and logico-metaphysical inquiries should be construed as accommodating the evidential inquiry. Our view of Plato's dialectic of definitions, which we treated in chapter 2, provides for the mutual accommodation of these various inquiries, including that of the *Meno*. Seen in this way, the distinction between acquaintance and description resists assimilation to those between being and becoming or is and seems and rather serves as an independent standpoint for examining philosophical problems and contributions to them. In particular, as we show further below, we have found that the paragenics of the *Meno* provides a helpful outlook on contemporary thought—certainly one closer to the spirit of recent thought than the ideal perspective of the *Republic*.

Twentieth-century thought is marked by great variety: pragmatisms, positivisms, phenomenologies, existentialisms, analytics, naturalisms, speculative metaphysics, and all the rest. Yet there is a sense of unity amid this diversity and we believe that paragenics provides a basis for studying this unity and for recognizing its philosophical cogency. At the same time, we discern many elements not paragenic in contemporary thought. In this chapter we extend the conception of paragenics from what we have found in the *Meno* to what may be called general paragenics (sec. i), and then briefly examine the theoretical (sec. ii and iii), and practical (sec. iv) aspects of general paragenics in the light of selected contributions from twentieth-century thought.

(i)   *The* Meno *and General Pragenics*

In this section we try to justify the enlargement of the notion of general paragenics from the more limited conception of paragenics found in the *Meno*. Our argument will be in two steps.

The Achievements and Limitations of the Meno. We have suggested already that the paragenics of the *Meno* centers upon acquisition—the vital human impulse of projecting oneself into the world and of acquiring valued objects both intellectual and practical. This vitality is shown in the uninhibited *ad hoc* questioning and answering of sophistic "wisdom," the inventiveness of Empedoclean poetic physical theory, the ingenuity of problem-solving in geometry, and the celebrated enterprise of Athenian policies. Taken by themselves such achievements appear questionable. Sophistic wisdom leads to verbal display; poetic physicalism is merely popular cosmology; geometric models are mind-teasers; Athenian policies are liable to reductions that turn them into opportunistic gambles, routine power plays, and misguided dependence on traditions. In dialogues other than the *Meno*, Plato often attacks these dubious features of sophistry or other undialectical pursuits, and then goes on to assimilate them into his dialectical and utopian structures. This obviously subordinates these pursuits to broader metaphysical principles. In the *Meno*, however, Plato avoids such assimilations. Within the inquiry, he looks at the undialectical pursuits and their achievements as characteristic human activities generating their own values. The *Meno* of course, does not ignore the faults to which they are liable; for example, the emptiness of eristic and the repression of ordinary politics. These features give way, however, before the more positive values which paragenics discovers and secures in them; for example, in finally answering Meno's first question without having a definition Socrates uses Gorgias' random order. Similarly, mathematics and politics are shown in paradigmatic though circumscribed form. Paragenics secures these positive values by using the notion of man as acquisitive to provide a unifying center for his diverse, open, and vital activities, and to give them substantive meaning. By this means the *Meno* establishes the compatibility of two properties often at odds in an idealistic philosophy: unmetaphysical novelty and cognitive certifiability. In thought, this compatibility is shown in the completeness of any "piece" of piecemeal knowledge which, because of its completeness, does not need to blend into a wider horizon (*Phaedrus*) or to provide an anticipation of the good reminiscent of the prisoners in the cave (*Republic* VII). The knowledge is both novel and hard. In practice, this compatibility is shown by the double fact that, on the one hand, Athenian policy-making was innovative or unsystematic and, on the other, the policies or public figures behind them were subject to definite judgments as virtuous or not. Thus the two goals envisaged in the *Meno* are, theoretically, the advancement of knowledge by inquiry, a knowledge which is self-sufficient and, practically, the advancement of individual and social freedom. We hazard that the latter is primary.

The *Meno*'s paragenics is nonetheless limited, not in its core or main divisions, but in its development. Its limitations are understandable, for it is but one of many works, all of them differing from each other. And there were limits on the innovations available in Plato's day. Geometrical discoveries were important but were still intricately bound up with the physical aspects of space (all nature is akin and cognitively available), and social problems were framed within the limitations of the city-state. Plato, therefore, does not emphasize the indefinite expansion of knowledge or even of freedom. Within the broad outline of his dialectic of definition, Plato used paragenics to locate the special problem of the practical acquisition of virtue, pointed toward action, guided by opinion. Such an inquiry might urge the Athenians to undertake a cultural and political revival after their defeat in the Peloponnesian war and after Socrates' execution.

General Paragenics as Derived from the Meno. General paragenics extends the paragenics of the *Meno* into a total philosophy concerned, as we shall see, with the full range of practical problems, such as the notions of justice, equality, freedom, the relation of thought to action, and so forth. Moreover, it adapts the division between acquaintance and description to clarify present epistemological distinctions, to simplify issues, and to help provide a unifying outlook. It emphasizes the inherent limitations in our knowing the *grounds* of knowing and of action.

General paragenics thus has a purgative effect, ridding philosophy of ideologically generated entities. From this standpoint, the dialectical substructure of the *Meno* shows Plato's reservation about the dialogue's reliance on existential evidence and opinion—a reservation which general paragenics does not share. Plato lacked the knowledge (supplied since his day) which could have shown him the scope of cognitive acquisitions man could develop in an intellectually open environment. The spirit of general paragenics is found in its grasp of the scope of a philosophy based on recognizing the compatibility between the novel and the hard. The recognition constitutes the essence of the piecemeal approach.

Because of limitations in the *Meno* and corresponding limitations of the innovative elements it dealt with, Plato did not concentrate on any one part of the total paragenic structure. It is easy to give disproportionate emphasis when any one part becomes so rich both in basic insights and in accumulated, validated opinions. Lacking these, Plato quite rightly concentrated on developing an overview in which several paragenic methods are distinguished and analogies among them are exploited.

General paragenics shares this outline with the *Meno*, but fills it in with such insights as can be borrowed from many branches of contemporary thought. It strives to maintain a balanced view of philosophy and its interrelated problems. General paragenics also recognizes in contemporary philosophies shortcomings caused by an essential one-sidedness. Because paragenic-like philosophies may be unbalanced in numerous ways, they lose the combined virtues of novelty (openness) and hardness (cognitive certifiability). We will later give instances of philosophies which are paragenic but fail because they are unbalanced. We trace virtually all such divergences from general paragenics, to a single source: failure to grasp the fact that unique conceptual and experiential links constitute causes, directly given in knowledge by acquaintance which in turn produce all opinions.

The paragenic stance tells us that when any particular problem is encountered it needs to be properly isolated, its parts separately dealt with in accord with the theoretic or practical elements involved, and the total complex cognitively encompassed within the flexible but significant criteria which the paragenic frame allows. In this way the particular inquiry determines its own direction, for paragenics allows no one-sided presumptions, no procrustean beds upon which to stretch or mutilate any issue. General paragenics is emphatically a philosophy, but—equally emphatically—it is not doctrinaire.

(ii)   *Paragenic Principles in Twentiety-Century Epistemology*

Bertrand Russell introduced his distinction between knowledge by acquaintance and knowledge by description early in the twentieth century.[1] Most of the subsequent talk about this distinction has been restricted to his conception of it.[2] In particular it has centered upon his notion of acquaintance knowledge of sense-data,[3] a notion which has been variously interpreted and has generated much controversy.[4] In the process, the word *acquaintance* becomes narrowed at one extreme and at another is extended to numbers,[5] and to religious, aesthetic, and existentialist experiences.[6] Such controverted interpretations are of little concern here so far as they could help to pinpoint Russell's particular view of acquaintance knowledge, but are useful as suggesting that an enlarged notion of knowledge by acquaintance underlies and even constitutes a common principle for twentieth-century philosophy. This suggestion is illustrated by G. E. Hughes' very perceptive treatment of Russell's notion of acquaintance knowledge.[7] Hughes finds an important comparison between acquaintance-theorists (such as Russell) and idealists (such as F. H. Bradley). For Bradley, experience is an act of judgment in which an ideal predicate detached from the flow of reality is reattached to reality which is the subject of all judgments.[8] An immediate experience is a noncognitive feeling from which discursive knowledge develops and leads to the completed act of judgment.[9] Thus an immediate basis of feeling or cognition (acquaintance) appears to underlie much twentieth-century philosophy. This notion applies as much to the basic sense-data experiences upon which the old protocol sentences of early positivism rest as it does to the variety of notions about immediate experience found in the philosophies of such thinkers as William James, John Dewey, Edmund Husserl, George Santayana, Jean-Paul Sartre, and A. N. Whitehead. These philosophies, though built upon different conceptions of acquaintance, extend descriptively into "conceptions of the world" which include the constructions of Russell and the positivists, the reconstruction of Husserl, the biological-cultural matrix of Dewey, the pluralistic universe of James, the metaphysics of events and enduring objects of Whitehead, and the projected world of Sartre.

For some philosophers, descriptions in a properly formalized language constitute adequately formulated knowledge, and no basis in prior acquaintance knowledge appears to be needed. The structure, as understood by experts, constitutes knowledge as distinct from unorganized opinion. In other cases, philosophy is primarily commonsense description of a world adequate for communication about observable entities—for example, a descriptive metaphysics of spatiotemporal bodies and persons with properties of various kinds and interacting in various ways.[10] For paragenics, these organized descriptions are warranted opinions.

For those philosophies in which acquaintance is an immediate noncognitive experience, descriptive discursive cognitions arise as consciousness of self and the object emerges from undifferentiated immediate experience.[11] The character of the feeling-stage and the subsequent stage of experience is conceived in many ways by various philosophies of experience and process: as acts of animal faith (Santayana), of inquiry (Dewey), of projection (Sartre), of intention (Husserl), of synaesthetic perception (Merleau-Ponty), of judgment (Bradley), of prehensive concrescence (Whitehead). These descriptions generally overlap and supplement each other.

The paragenic principle of distinguishing acquaintance from description thus pervades much twentieth-century thought, although the principle appears in many places and has been used in conjunction with unlike philosophic methods. In contrast to those for whom acquaintance is of logically prior atomic sense-data, general paragenics emphasizes the causally ordered structure of knowledge by acquaintance, a complex but logically first ground of all cognition. This determination is in agreement with the idealistic conception such as we meet in followers of Bradley, that knowledge must be discursive even though it conflicts with their notion that acquaintance itself is noncognitive. General paragenics in this way emphasizes both the discursive structure of knowledge and its direct givenness. It rejects the notion that noncognitive immediate experience is philosophically basic and finds that our fully conscious acts of knowing (from the conceptual to the experiential) are paradigms for all experience, that is, it treats the vaguer, less conscious "immediate experiences" in terms of our sharply defined acts of knowledge by acquaintance.

In addition to rejecting atomic sense-data and immediate noncognitive experience as constituting acquaintance, general paragenics also rejects the conception of causality, on the one hand, as created by repeated experiences of conjoined pairs of similar objects, and on the other, as an outcome of an "internal adventure of becoming."[12] For general paragenics therefore, causality is found not in the psychological generation of habits or in some metaphysical grounds of process; instead, the causal structure of each act of knowing by acquaintance is unique and of a kind suited to the conditions and consequences which the cause links. The theoretical structure of general paragenics is its very epistemology. The objects of this are immediate ingredients of acquaintance knowledge.

(iii)   *The Epistemology of General Paragenics*

Most of our cognitions are mixtures of acquaintance knowledge and descriptive opinions. Only such persons as a witness in a judicial proceeding or a philosopher seeking epistemological precision have occasion sharply to separate knowledge from opinion. We make such a separation now.

Acquaintance Knowledge. Acquaintance knowledge is not immediate or prior in a temporal sense, but it is logically prior as the cognition of causal structures from which further descriptive cognitions are derivable. In the *Meno*, Plato distinguished four kinds of this knowledge: conceptual, artistic, factual, and entitative. This last includes knowledge of persons—for example, Meno—of places, and of things. We have examined the first three in some detail in chapters 3, 5 and 6, and 7. Our purpose here is not to summarize but to make explicit the derivations from as well as the limits implicit in each of the four kinds.

a) *Conceptual Discovery.* The theoretical paradigm for all knowledge is the discovery of a causal connection between concepts: one square and another double its area, for example. The discovery establishes a self-substantiated conceptual structure, a known particular whole which is a part of the mind of the knower. Universal laws applicable to particular instances are derivable from such a discovery; for instance, that from any square, a square double in area may be drawn on its diagonal. The derivation is a universal generalization from a known particular. Similarly, from any discovered identity within a theoretical structure—for example, "heat is molecular motion (properly specified)"—one may derive a universal—"All heat is molecular motion (properly specified)."[13] Additional properties about squares may be conjectured descriptively and later justified by discovery; for example, that the side and diagonal of a square are incommensurable.

Such ideas are innate, not in the sense that they have a privileged and formative role with respect to other ideas,[14] but in the sense that constituting a part of man's mind, they have vividness, exactness, and autonomy in contrast with the routine, dull, imprecise notions of ordinary thought. Discovery itself defies systematic explanation, though one may know retrospectively the facts surrounding an individual discovery and though the conceptual relationship, while *sui generis,* is available to all prepared minds. Attempts to explain discovery yield suggestive myths—not knowledge. Poincaré's description of discovery as activating atomic ideas hanging on the walls of the mind[15] contrasts interestingly with Plato's poetic, priestly tale of reminiscence and rebirth of souls. The latter treats the mind not as an empty bag but as a complex whole, only partially accessible to man at a given time, though larger portions become increasingly available to men. Such myths are descriptive extensions, not knowledge.

b) *Artistic Knowledge.* We know directly by acquaintance, arts, skills, habits, or dispositions. These modes of knowing are established responses to given sets of circumstances and yield specified valued ends. The point of interest is not the individual action but the way of acting. Such ways are causes that connect prior conditions with achievable outcomes and thus yield a particular whole known by acquaintance. We establish knowledge of the way (knowing how) by repeating similar action. A form or rule of action develops from relatively haphazard responses of prior unformed actions.

Such rules are not completely determinative of an action. Differences in circumstances, in instruments, in possible combinations of rules, in envisaged ends, and so forth, occasion new opinions about the way to act, thereby introducing new rules and novel methods of action. Thus, the indeterminacy in applying rules is a source of novelty and creativity.

One sometimes speaks of the "truth" of an art object, but the proper way to speak is of objects well or poorly made, or produced by skills of high or low quality. The "truth" of an art object then refers to the consistency of the parts contributing to a unified end. Of course, one may give true or false descriptions about arts.

Rules can be shared and they are eminently teachable. The primary social rules are those of language arts. Subtleties in the rules for language use are generally hidden by their one-dimensional structure as a system of symbols or sounds.[16] Though there is indeterminacy in usage as well as in all rule-governed behavior,[17] regularities in common usage are codified by grammarians, and rules of word usage, sentence-formation and transformation are clearly specified in scientific discourse.

c) *Knowledge of Particular Fact.* The core of knowledge by acquaintance of particular fact is a completed experience, as we argued in chapter 7. It is not conceptual discovery (the material for which is drawn from experience), or knowing how (which is built upon experience). Habitual knowledge and factual knowledge are distinct but related. Habits are acquired and exercised in actions; conversely, all actions consist in part of some regularities of response. As rules of art allow innovation in particular applications, so novelty in decision-making is normally guided by past known regularities. Completed experiences are the standard for understanding the less clear, routine, and involuntary as well as the abortive and fragmentary experiences. Experiences vary in duration; they overlap and interlock. But experience is just as it occurs and just as men act. But although we may be wrong prospectively and bring about effects we do not want, although we may remember badly and misstate facts, and although we may misinterpret what happens before our own eyes, experience is irretrievably and incorrigibly acquaintance knowledge. One may of course concentrate on portions of an experience—whether these be relatively substantial entities or more fleeting "events" such as houses, wagons, hills, sounds, flashes of light, odors, as we shall note below.

   d) *Knowledge of Empirical Entities* (persons, places, and things). Plato introduced the notion of acquaintance knowledge by making the analogy between our knowing virtue and our knowing Meno as good-looking, rich, and well-born. Clearly, knowledge of persons, places, and things emerges from our knowledge of particular facts. By knowing the road from Athens to Larisa and from Athens to Delphi, and so forth, we come to know at least the location of Athens. Similarly, by observing Meno exercise ownership of property, clip coupons, live in luxury, and so forth, we know that he is rich. Thus one knows empirical entities as one interacts with them or observes their own interaction with circumstances. Some entities are relatively stable and repeatedly identifiable in similar interlocking experiences. Though the knowing is like a habit or customary conjunction, as Hume maintained, what is known is not a habit but an object—and not an object created out of impressions, but isolated from the context of experience. The object's identity and singularity is known by acquaintance as previous memories of experiences of the object in a common framework merge with current experiences of it. Objects thus have identifiable properties, some more stable than others, but all are modes of response to circumstances in which objects interact. Our knowledge of such entities is limited to what is directly experienced. For example, of a person we know only the evidential skills, conceptual achievements, and shared factual experiences (including the regularities exhibited by such persons); but such knowledge does not extend to what one is merely told about a person, and certainly not to the existential indeterminacies of a person facing unfamiliar situations with unknown or perhaps (at a given moment) even nonexistent resources. In this sense of our knowing objects, astronomers in the thirteenth and twentieth centuries see and know by acquaintance the same object when they see a sunrise,[18] despite the facts a) that our cognition that it is the same object is an opinion by description (we do not have the knowledge by acquaintance which the thirteenth-century astronomers had) and b) that the theoretical grasp of the sunrise in the two cases differ—the later being enriched by conceptual discoveries subsequent to the earlier perception. Certainly, the repeatability of similar perceptions in diverse experiential contexts generates our notion of a relatively stable world with identifiable entities about which we theorize in so many ways.

Descriptive Cognitions. "Our notion of a relatively stable world" consists of acquaintance knowledge of the four kinds discussed above, supplemented by descriptive opinions extending beyond such knowledge. The very mixture of acquaintance and descriptive cognitions provides a context in which our knowledge increases and our bases for action are broadened. Thus, starting from the original knowledge of the double-square solution, men have asked about or described the problem of comparing the lengths of the diagonal and side of a given square, have discovered that the two are incommensurable, and have been led further to discover the general principles of proportionality applicable to the ordering of magnitudes. Or again, from our observations of a friend's abilities we may surmise how he will respond to new challenges, and subsequently observe an extra capability which he reveals under the new circumstances.

In general paragenics, there are two modes of descriptive extensions of acquaintance knowledge: a) commonsense descriptions and b) scientific descriptions.

a) *Commonsense Descriptions.* Commonsense descriptions are extensions (generalizations and projections into the future) from our acquaintance knowledge of the arts, of facts, and of empirical objects. Our description of our world as a complex of entities, events, and facts in which we and other persons act and acquire habits of response is thus a highly generalized opinion, large portions of which are commonly shared and only small portions of which are known by acquaintance. The total picture undergoes repeated correction and refinement. There are many philosophical descriptions of this common world, each emphasizing particular aspects as central. General paragenics accepts such descriptions as overlapping accounts of this world, readily accommodates descriptive cognitions of reasonable beliefs about our world, and rejects tendentious universal doubts as less than reasonable.[19]

The self is the total of experienced feelings, achievements, cognitions, acquired in interaction with objects and other persons in the world, as well as one's own recognized indeterminacies as one faces ever-new situations.[20] Such indeterminacy is not merely lack of knowledge in a world presumed to be strictly determined, nor is it more than suggestively associated with the quantum indeterminacy of recent physical theory.[21] Though acting and experiencing is the ground for freedom of choice, there is no evidence for a "free will" or a mental spirit. Consciousness is merely a function of selves in which they reflect on feelings, actions, and cognitions. No "mental spirit" is derivable from such a function.

b) *Scientific Descriptions.* The paradigms of scientific descriptions are the highly theoretical explanations of physics in which previously discovered causes provide the organizing structure and the theoretic links. The directly experienced physical necessity of starting at a given point and taking a specified path to another desired point may be described abstractly and generalized by appropriate notations for position, direction, units of distance, mass moved, time elapsed, speed variations, energy consumed, and so forth. Discovery of causes as links in the abstract relations between the fundamental physical parameters derives from an experiential basis, but is conceptually or theoretically self-substantiated independently of that basis. Such links are applicable to instances of further experiences. Establishing and applying the conceptual links require many skills of laboratory and symbolic manipulation. Thus, scientific cognitions are complex descriptive extensions from all four kinds of acquaintance knowledge. The paradigm of physical necessity is the completed experienced fact and the paradigm of physical cognition is conceptual discovery of causes. However, the paradigm of scientific description is the covering-law argument,[22] though this is only a part of the total structure of cognitions constituting science.

Predicting the outcome of an experiment by using the covering-law argument constitutes a descriptive opinion about the future which may or may not be confirmed. Disconfirmation of such an opinion indicates that the conceptual discoveries underlying the descriptive hypotheses are not operative in the physical necessities which obtain in the completed, known results of the experiment. This misfit may be traceable to any one of the several elements intrinsic to the cognitive structure governing the theory or to deficiencies in experimental practice. A scientific explanation is thus a descriptive structure, including the constructions and inferences built from notions adopted as primary. Theories of scientific explanation vary from the logical inquiries into the syntactical, semantical, and pragmatic elements used in science to the "life-like" experiential inquiries comprising the context of the history of science.[23]

Commonsense and scientific descriptive regularities are made up of many types of cognitions. The physical world is a conjoined series of events allowing indefinite conceptual and experiential expansion. There is no incompatibility of descriptive regularities with freedom to choose and act on the basis of one's opinion of what is best under given circumstances. This compatibility in no way erases the highly validated regularities, for the prospective view of action cannot be made to conflict with known actual facts, discovered conceptual relations, or descriptive generalities derived from them. The full implications of these epistemological distinctions for the problems of the relation between mind and body and of freedom and determinism must be left to a future occasion, though some indication of them will be suggested in the line of argument immediately following.

(iv)   *Practical Paragenics*

Practical paragenics is the study of man acquiring goods. Man as acquisitive is identifiable by the kinds of objects he acquires and by the modes of acquisition. His capacity to choose, act, and obtain what he values—personal and social, theoretical and practical—under given circumstances, is governed by his understanding of the situation. His cognition is itself a value as well as an intrinsic element in each experience. As we noted earlier, acquaintance knowledge is a theoretical acquisition from which descriptive cognition is in turn elicited.

In chapter 6 we presented the practical principles of the *Meno* as based on a conception of human good which is neither systematic nor relativist, one in which the best obtainable society is not a utopia fixed to some ideal conception but a society of consent in which men are free to seek goods they need or want. We extend this conception in general paragenics and take note of the fact that much contemporary practical philosophy is strongly paragenic. Current practice suggests we treat two areas: the theory of action and political theory.

Theory of Action. In ethical theories such as G. E. Moore's intuitionism,[24] R. M. Hare's prescriptivism,[25] and Charles L. Stevenson's emotivism,[26] the good is nonrelativistic, valued as felt, identifiable but not knowable, and constituted of real connections of a magnitude and complexity not available to man as knowledge. But these thinkers severally argue for 1) the separation of fact from value, 2) the avoidance of naturalistic fallacies, 3) the appeal to persuasive intent or prescriptions as distinct from scientific descriptions. Practical paragenics does not attempt to derive value from fact, because it recognizes that facts as given and our knowledge of them have been derived from human actions in which valuation and judgment are primary.

Although there is no knowledge of an ultimate human good and man's appropriate action for acquiring it, there are many opinions about human action—such opinions having been generalized from various aspects of individual actions. Paragenic principles of action appear in diverse treatments of problems such as those of freedom and determinism, the relation of thought to action, the language used to describe action ("will," "intention," etc.). In contemporary formulations these principles are accommodated sometimes to a Humean conception of causality and sometimes to a dialectic structure of thought. We briefly review a selection of the vast literature on this subject.

J. L. Austin's analysis of the meaning of "ifs" and "cans" as they are used in statements such as "I can if I choose," appears to give linguistic support to the paragenic conception of man's freedom to choose in acting to acquire human good. Austin argues that the clauses "I can" and "if I choose" cannot be taken as two separate clauses in a normal conditional sentence.[27] He suggests a conclusion that though "determinism itself is still a name for nothing clear," his arguments about "ifs" and "cans" "fail to show that it [determinism] *is* true, and indeed in failing go some way to show that it is *not*. Determinism appears not consistent with what we ordinarily say and presumably think."[28]

Doubtless one can interpret "can . . . if" and "could . . . if" sentences as normal conditionals and construe human action within a deterministic frame of laws, as P. H. Nowell-Smith and others seem to suggest.[29] Austin, however, appears to describe our language usage more accurately and presents a more concrete account of our actual experiences in acting. Austin's cautiously framed conclusion about the inconsistency of determinism "with what we ordinarily say and presumably think" is further supported by Arthur C. Danto's arguments, which are developed in line with the context of a Humean causal model, for the necessity of noncaused basic action.[30] General paragenics, derived as it is from the *Meno*, is clearly committed to an indeterminism in the prospective view of action, while at the same time it recognizes the necessities which obtain in completed actions and in lawlike description or hypotheses.

Our freedom to choose in no way conflicts with H. L. A. Hart and A. M. Honore's causal concept "latent in ordinary thought,"[31] that actions are explained by reasons, the explanatory force of which comes from within the particular case. Explanations are answers to "questions primarily about the agent's experience in contemplating, deciding upon, and carrying out the action in question."[32] The particular connection between reason and action is thus known retrospectively in the completed experience of it. Hart and Honore reject any prospective view of action, excluding "foreseeability" as a proposed alternative to a causal analysis.[33]

Paragenics, on the other hand, is concerned with the prospective as well as the retrospective views of action and in particular with the foresight of competent political leaders.[34] As we have noted, moreover, the paragenic account allows the covering-law model to apply to actions as a derivative generalized non-causal description, thus using a universal hypothesis for stating the regularities of past actions appropriate for explaining a given case.[35]

Stuart Hampshire gives a prospective view of action as he determines that man is an intentionally active being capable of choosing,[36] and he also adds that even retrospectively, one may never know the "real causes" of an action.[37] He believes that the connection between thought and action is "altogether mysterious,"[38] and that man's actions become freer as his knowledge becomes fuller.[39] Thus, though Hampshire grounds his conceptions on the paragenic principle of man as actively choosing on the basis of his opinion of what is best, he misses the retrospective acquaintance knowledge of causally ordered actions. Further, in holding that fuller knowledge increases man's freedom, he seems to be appealing to a nonparagenic, quite idealistic conception of freedom and knowledge.

Paul Ricoeur has well expressed a nonparagenic conception of human action and freedom. Moving from the external opposition of man versus nature to an internal process of action seen from the standpoint of "practical mediation"[40] (as distinct from man's cognitive and affective nature[41]), he argues the reciprocal opposition of the voluntary and involuntary elements at every stage, from decision through action to consent. This makes the issue not one of diametrically opposed concepts but one of accommodating contraries. Thus Ricoeur internalizes a comprehensive context, social and physical, used as the background for analyzing action, in which opposing "forces" (e.g., internal motives and external necessities) operate reciprocally to "produce" voluntarily and involuntarily the objects, actions, and feelings making up man's existence and his significance. Such a comprehensive dialectical structure appears to lack the precision and evidential character so important for coming to grips with the details of human action.

In addition, such a treatment of human action raises the question of what description of the limits and of the sort of unity in actions may serve as paradigms for understanding it. On the one hand, "turning out a light by flipping an electric switch" seems an inadequate paradigm, and on the other hand, Herodotus' description of the deeds of Gyges and Croesus and their consequences (see chap. 7) seems over-inclusive. Ricoeur's conception of the paradigm as an "initial pathos . . . recovered in a theory of praxis"[42] in a never-completed philosophical anthropology, appears closer to the (to us) unacceptable case of Gyges. The real paradigm for paragenics is a man formulating opinions about, and acting to acquire, the thing or things he deems best for himself under given circumstances. And the normal treatment of the outcomes of previous actions as major factors in these present circumstances is basic in the longer-span continuity of action.

This paradigm of man's acquiring goods involves no special attitudes or objects described naturalistically. Man does not merely react subjectively nor does he merely calculate logistically. He acquires what is appropriate to himself, ranging from material goods to religious experience, and these goods may include habits as achieved values, both those in which ends are prescribed (Aristotle's courage, for instance) and those relatively neutral as to ends (Benjamin Franklin's perseverance or early-to-bed habit).

There is no preset standard to guide man's action; neither a transcendent principle, a principle in human nature, nor a calculus of pleasure over pain. Final truths about all men, such as Karl Jaspers' ultimate situation[43] or Sartre's existential burden,[44] do not figure here, despite man's uncertainty in searching for and acquiring values, and, of course, the certainty of death. Man is only acquiring (or failing to acquire) the particular goods he seeks in given circumstances, which include the association with others for common goals within political communities.

Paragenic Political Theory. As we said earlier, paragenic political theory rejects ideal utopias, though such a rejection should not be taken as justifying Robert Nozick's minimal state.[45] Paragenics equally, however, rejects the anarchic principles of man and society which are the explanatory grounds of such a minimal state. Paragenics appeals to tradition rather than to a rational explanatory basis. A controversy between Alexander Bickel and Richard Wasserstrom on whether the United States Supreme Court can deal systematically with social problems is suggestive.

Bickel's position is that political virtue is rooted in tradition but as a guide to adaptive change. He argues that the magnitude, complexities, and general ramifications of social problems makes it best for society to proceed in an empirical way, based on its traditions.[46]

Wasserstrom argues in opposition that he fails to understand why anyone rejects rational systematic efforts to solve social problems.[47]

Wasserstrom must be granted that wholesale arguments against rational efforts to cure evil are foolish, yet Bickel speaks of specific ills in definite times and places and cures that carry with them all the aforementioned difficulties of setting priorities and of dealing with concrete weakness in applying systematic deductive methods. The more rigorous the methods become, the more they underplay the necessities for empirical tests which Wasserstrom does not regard as persuasive.

Certainly political virtue in Plato's *Republic* and B. F. Skinner's *Walden Two*[48] is systematic and teachable, for the state as a construct is made up of a finite and exhaustive set of circumstances. Paragenics, on the contrary, finds that determinate boundaries are not available in an existential situation. Not only are the facts without limit; the number of sets of categories in terms of which they are analyzable is similarly open. Bickel's position emphasizes this.

Paragenics begins, then, with existing states and their traditions. States assure the material and cultural conditions for action. Such conditions are neither value-neutral nor value-prescriptive, but are adapted to the preservation of already achieved values and to the encouragement of the pursuit of new ones in changing circumstances. Working, successful societies are therefore both open to and helpful in guiding men in their search for new values. The prevalence of this conception of the state is widely in evidence. For example, the United States Constitution justifies its patent and copyright provision not merely as protecting property but also as promoting the progress of science and useful arts. Or again, Theodore Roosevelt solicited the commitment of different groups to broad national purposes on the ground that he had first taken into account their right to pursue their particular self-interest.[49] Thus, the state provides a continuing but changing sphere for action in which citizens locate ends and achieve happiness individually and in groups. Tradition, circumstances, and human choices determine groupings and functions. Happiness consists not only of terminal satisfactions which actions bring, but also, as in any commonsense view, in reasonably warranted hopes for the future of the individual and of society.

Various theories emphasize various aspects of humans and their relations in society, from the welfare theories which are based on the utilitarian credo of maximizing satisfactions, to the contract theories which in turn are based on mutual rights and obligations of individuals in the just distribution of goods. Thus for John Rawls "in justice as fairness the concept of right is prior to that of good."[50] Utilitarians reverse this priority; and however slight the difference in consequences, the opposition in principle is vigorous. Paragenics avoids issues of priority, recognizing that different concepts may provide complementary insights into concrete issues.

Hume placed social relations between close family relationships (full mutual benevolence) and relations among entities not sharing a common structure (rapacious individualism). Social theories of right or of welfare are applicable only within the middle region, for here rational discourse, useful in pressing or rebutting claims and in seeking adjudication when they conflict, is open to the citizens. In Hume's analysis, utility and justice are not opposed.[51] Paragenics borrows from Hume and also agrees with Nicholas Rescher's conception of the "due meshing of considerations of justice . . . with those of utility,"[52] though our method differs from that of the latter.

Even within the concept of justice, paragenics gives play to existent diversity. Rawls accords priority to numerical equality, liberty, and the model of equals making a "bargain."[53] He abstracts from the empirical frame, sets up an ideal theory assuming "strict compliance,"[54] and treats the political problem as being that of exploiting every circumstance for bringing society closer to that ideal. Robert Nozick, however, argues for an entitlement theory of distributive justice in which men justly hold what is appropriated from things not owned or acquired by transfer from another who is entitled to the holding.[55] Nozick's chief point is that taxation for any purpose other than the maintenance of the minimum state, that is, a state providing protection from or compensation for injuries, is an unjust redistribution of the holdings of men rightfully entitled to their possessions. For him, there is no defensible pattern or ideal of distribution, but rather, men acquire and hold what is justly gained by risk-taking, by work, by gifts, and the like.

For paragenics, there is no man-to-man equality or other ideal distributive pattern. No single human activity can adequately serve as a paradigm for justice in all the circumstances in which men interact in a fully developed society, whether one thinks of trading on an equal basis, of mixing one's labor with materials, of risk-taking, of associating for monopolistic purposes, or any other activities and conditions. Proportional equality (as distinct from numerical equality), and the corresponding fruits of merit or aggressiveness, can be accorded an independent status. The problem is less one of demonstrating that everyone benefits (Rawls) than it is of recognizing the obligations of all within a state to participate freely and with expectations of due rewards for their contributions to the general welfare. This point applies equally to circumstances where invisible hands might produce equilibriums (Nozick) which would effectively eliminate from the system individuals who could contribute and actively participate. Again, while the standard of need is proper under some conditions, such a standard or a rule of proportionate equality would be ridiculous in the just administration of a lottery.

We have mentioned several convergent ways in which paragenics treats the conception and role of justice; but the foundation for paragenics is an actual state-in-being that provides the setting for man's acquisitive activities. The setting is the total network of accrued values common and individual, with their recent histories and the implications of these histories for a continuity of acquired values and of projected new enterprises, national and individual. Justice is the result of past contributions to society determining the distribution of values, taken with the emerging forces (individuals or groups) making their contributions at present, and getting their share of rewards without unduly prejudicing the prospects of possible future contributors.

An individual sees justice for himself as a socially conditioned, warranted claim; it is a right to something on the basis of law, custom, or even a rising public sense as the basis for a public claim. It is no mere inner satisfaction; justice even includes an effort to change the basis of claims. No single doctrine of fairness, entitlement, and so forth, can serve as a completely satisfactory formula for this concept. This statement itself is not a set formula, though its significance may be delineated in light of what the best societies throughout history have produced. Each state must provide laws—themselves subject to change—which make adjustments of the forces within society possible. There are many possibilities of failure—failure of justice, enterprise, conditions of opportunity, and the public sense of these failures. Issues are those of the maintenance, renewal, and change of accrued powers and opportunities; and these are confronted in terms of specific problems, not of movement toward a comprehensive end.

This paragenic principle which we have just now enunciated is that of man's acquiring goods, though goods in a broad sense. Providing the conditions of freedom to appreciate accrued values and to invent and project new ends-in-view drawn from present resources constitutes the primary political function. The action of acquiring and maintaining the well-being of a society requires leadership as well as consensus. We said earlier that there is no fixed principle which can serve to guide leaders in their decisions on matters affecting the well-being of large numbers of men. Society must at the very least provide the condition for open discussion of values—their diversity, their compatibility or incompatibility, their manifesting of possibilities for acting in new ways, and so on. Only such conditions can produce the men needed for leadership and enable the society to recognize and select them for such service. Maintaining these conditions of freedom of discourse without splitting the society into warring factions on the one hand, or allowing some dominant faction to get control and institute a repressive government on the other, is, of course, a matter for continuing inquiry and for sharp vigilance in society. This is the central concern for paragenic political philosophy.

This brief sketch has dealt for the most part with some of the ways in which numberless insights in contemporary practical philosophy may be accommodated within a broad-based paragenic outlook. If we concentrate upon practical paragenic reasoning, we find three complementary methods. First is the hypothetical mode of establishing general rules, deducing the implications of such rules, and applying the rules and implications to particular cases. Some twentieth-century political thought is cast in this form. Second comes the search for guidance in the opinions of the experts or of men recognized as practically wise or of a consensus of the many through poll-taking, and so forth. Much social and political speculation is of this sort. And finally there is the sensitive determination of men of wide authority, facing crucial cases involving determinations which best fit a total context of ever-changing circumstances, including attitudes of the men they must persuade. If these men repeatedly produce choices we retrospectively know to have been right, they truly have the power of persuasive reasoning which is ultimate practical wisdom.

(v)   *Paragenics: A Perennial Philosophy of Limits*

The burden of earlier sections in this chapter suggests that paragenic tendencies pervade much of contemporary thought despite the fact that these tendencies are generally mixed with others that paragenics would not accept. We list a few samples of such mixtures. In each case we have put first the insight which belongs to general paragenics, and have then indicated that the way its author failed to follow through paragenically is not merely a turn in the approach but a limitation of the original insight.

a) The importance of precision, for example, of isolating diverse conceptual regions, as Husserl argues.[56] For paragenics, however, these are identified with diverse kinds of causal connections and are not merely descriptive.

b) The identity of knower and known as indicated by the single point where two lines cross—the lines being the historical processes of each (knower and known) as James describes the immediate experience.[57] This description of knowledge by acquaintance is suggestive, though it misses the complex structure of the combined knower-known entity.

c) The necessity of internal relations interpreted as the bonds of knowledge by such men as Bradley and Whitehead,[58] but Bradley's appeal to experience as an act of judgment, and Whitehead's conception of process as prehensive unification, both give a generalized logical and organic account which neglects the uniqueness and causally self-constituted character of acquaintance knowledge.

d) The notion of an empirical "cause" as for Dewey,[59] a cause which is neither a force "pushing" events nor a final end "pulling" events into line, but a historical link in a series of actions. Unfortunately, Dewey's commitment to action prevents him from seeing that the unity of the historical series is modeled on causally unified conceptual relations.

3) The emphasis Bergmann gives to acts of awareness or acquaintance.[60] On the other side, he neglects their complex self-substantiating structure, grounding his analysis on an ideal language, an interpreted syntactical schema.

f) Popper's conception of the logic of scientific discovery as the testing of falsifiable hypotheses and of the openness of society as an ideal.[61] The first is essentially an alternative way of accounting for scientific description and misses the centrality of conceptual discovery as self-constituted knowledge; and the second misses the centrality of leadership in social advance.

g) The perspicuous representative function of language within the realm of action as for Wittgenstein,[62] who even so does not distinguish fundamentally different kinds of knowledge and opinion expressible in language.

h) The notion of a spatiotemporal frame for bodies and persons of a descriptive metaphysics.[63] This should be derived from the causal structure of experience which in turn rests on the insights available from conceptual discoveries.

i) The existentialist view of man as projecting himself into an unknown. Paragenics rejects the generalized dialectic associated with this view and treats the indeterminacy in a piecemeal manner.

j) James' and Whitehead's notion of a limited God, supportive of man's action.[64] Paragenic meliorism for its part is not founded upon a metaphysic of process, but is based on man's experiences of human advance.

These examples suggest principles and methods other than those of paragenics. In section iv above, we glanced at the way a Humean conception of causality and alternatively the way a dialectical structure of thought could be introduced into consideration of a theory of action. Such treatments have led to what in section i we termed a lack of balance. In its attempt to achieve concreteness even as it rejected both the psychologisms and abstractions of earlier philosophies, twentieth-century philosophy has commenced its analyses with the structure of language or experience or processes, all these having been conceived in many ways. The search for concreteness in these directions has brought with it the loss of the combined virtues of novelty (openness) and hardness (cognitive certifiability) which general paragenics makes fundamental. And the deviations from the balanced position has led to one or another of three possible deficiencies.

The First Direction: Philosophy is reduced to an attenuation or purgation of itself. It can find the errors in earlier philosophizing, but it has difficulty in identifying philosophical problems and in productively developing their significance. Much of the critical literature in linguistic analysis is of this sort. Many such thinkers have failed to work out constructive solutions to questions.

The Second Direction: Other paragenic-like contemporary philosophies have overemphasized the hardness and neglected the openness of piecemeal philosophies. Such philosophies arrogate to themselves the "hard" status of a science as they conceive it and presume all of philosophy must achieve this same status. Husserl's phenomenology claims to be a science of sciences—grounded in certainties, phenomenological ultimates.[65] Anticipations of total physical explanations, hoped for though not yet scientifically attained (we find these in Wilfrid Sellars), constitute another example of such "super-hardness."[66] This applies also to the "explanatory theories" that presume to be total philosophies, for these neglect the central source of all cognition in the data of conceptual discovery and of direct experiential acquaintance just completed. These philosophies instead find their "hardness" in extraneously derived abstract elements: egos, ultimate atomic particles, logical structure.

The Third Direction: Still other paragenic-like contemporary philosophies lose the hard character of either the conceptual or experiential knowledge, or both, by assimilating one to the other. Dewey, for one, underplays the uniqueness of conceptual discovery in his logic of inquiry and discovery, for in point of fact it is analyzable as a correlation of changes acquiring the honorific status of knowledge only in actional extensions.[67] Or again, Merleau-Ponty, emphasizing the figure-ground notion of perception as involving the intrinsic relationship of percipient and perceived in actions, reduces the hardness of both conceptual discovery and experience by treating perception as a paradoxical unity of dialectical contraries, for example, immanence and transcendence.[68]

Paragenics is an old word, which we are now using as a new name for a general philosophical position which encompasses many of the contributions found here and there in twentieth-century philosophy—in pragmatisms, phenomenologies, analytics, positivisms, existentialisms, and the others. Yet it is not eclectic, for its origin as a unified philosophy predates the manifold expressions of these contributions in the thought of today. It is therefore not new, but it is the modern effort to establish the minimal philosophy that can cogently repudiate both scepticism and the idols of speculation. Never before have the materials for such a philosophy been so rich and promising; but comparable attempts have been made repeatedly, especially in the paragenic-like systems centering on action, from the time of the sophists through such men as Cicero, Machiavelli, and Burke, right up to the present.

Although there is a common character to all these philosophies, each has a distinctive form answering to the dominating currents of its time. For present-day paragenics this means that a general philosophy of action and of mind is the result primarily of scientific cognition in at least two ways.[69] First, such cognition of the evolutions of stars, planets, and life forms suggests that the human species is a mere incident in the fortuitous concourse of physical, chemical, and biological forces. Clearly the existence of man and all life on earth may be ended by any one of an indefinite number of unexpected cataclysmic events. Yet man's gaining the power to destroy himself has terrorized him much more profoundly than his recognition of his fragility as a natural species. For the existence of man is now subject to mere whims, and the choice of leaders whose deficiencies formerly determined no more than the fate of a single nation can now determine the very existence of all mankind. Thus scientific certainties reinforce the human uncertainties in action.

Paragenics as a philosophy of the practical necessarily oriented to the new science, recognizes the need for hope in face of the increasing uncertainties of action. This is not Bacon's hope based on the notion that science, properly pursued, is the source of man's control over nature.[70] That control is now largely achieved and is still growing, but it has not solved the problems of life. Clearly, the proper uses of knowledge depend upon right opinion, as the *Meno* suggests. In these circumstances, where knowledge is not available, belief in some being who has thus far blessed mankind with gifted individuals seems not unreasonable, though such a belief is never knowledge. Dewey, Sartre, and others have emphasized man's insecurity.[71] William James has conceived of God as providing a basis of hope for men.[72] This belief is not a metaphysical argument for God's existence, nor can it justify reliance on magic and the occult. These beliefs really sketch the limits of human insight and power and form a support for human effort to attain the best that mankind can achieve for itself.

Besides the new bearing of science on the practical, the very magnitude and multiplicity of its discoveries, has enabled philosophy to form a more adequate conception of science, of its history, and of human cognitions. In early modern philosophy, a great scientific discovery generally inspired unified philosophies, as for example, the seventeenth-century use of the geometric method. Again there is the late nineteenth- and early twentieth-centuries' use of evolutionary theory.[73] However, the very diversity of problems and methods, of generalizations, and of conceptual discoveries in so many fields of inquiry has undermined the notion of science as a single ideal body of knowledge. It suggests instead that science is a loose-woven network of partly interlocked and partly disconnected concepts derived in various ways from variegated experiences. This emerging notion of science suggests a more flexible view of the history of science.[74] The emphasis is upon incremental additions to and subtractions from the network of opinions, validated with different degrees of assurance. Any such changes would involve, in different ways, other related elements in the total conjunction of cognitions. This emphasis on piecemeal elements within properly limited frames suggests how out of place are the appeals to overarching principles or dialectical structures, whether or not these be called "scientific." Thus scientific cognitions, both in their results and in their structures, suggest a paragenic conception of mind as well as of action.

Paragenics, as a philosophy of mind, accordingly surveys and relates the totality of man's cognitive achievements. It does not occupy a unique position as knowledge of a special sort distinct from cognitions acquired in other pursuits. Instead it retrospectively examines the structure and limits of our cognitions. It is not antiphilosophical; it is a minimum philosophy with clearly exposed assumptions and methods. However, the pervasiveness of paragenics as a leading mode of philosophizing through the twentieth century suggests at the same time the possibility that philosophy is moving in a new direction. Philosophy regularly breaks through modes of thought which have dominated its past.

As a perennial though minimal philosophy, paragenics serves as a standard against which much recent work may be measured. As such, it constitutes a philosophy of readiness, of possibilities for human action. And it provides a general framework for dealing with particular problems of all kinds—theoretical and practical. It is a systematized philosophy of everyday life.

Appendix　　Notes　　Index

Appendix

The argument in the *Meno* can be reduced to a matrix form in which pairs of terms govern the movement of thought from one stage to the next. Three illustrations or schemata will follow shortly, the second including the content of the first and the third including the content of the first and second. The first simply represents the initial search for a definition of virtue, and concludes with the agreement that one can get a single definition for the diverse virtues of men, women, and children. The second outlines the three parts of the section on definition—ending with virtue's being defined (unsuccessfully it happens) in terms of the just acquisition or nonacquisition of goods (wealth, etc.). In the third schema, the trichotomous pattern of the first two schemata is applied also to the structure of the dialogue as a whole. This trichotomous pattern recurs in the modes of discourse Plato specifies and in the total structure of the argument (see chap. 8, and sec. ii below).

These schemata merely summarize the content in outline form, and suggest two-dimensional dichotomies as governing the organization of this content. In the first schema, the two dichotomies are other-same and many-one; one organizing the subject matter, the other the way the problem is treated. In comparison, definitions two and three turn on species-genus (form-matter) and part-whole respectively, as indicated in the second schema of all the definitions. In the second schema, definition one has been collapsed to a single column (the left), with three stages. Similarly schemata for definitions two and three collapse to form the middle and right-hand columns of the schema for the whole definitional section. The guiding dichotomies appear in different fashion; for example, the many-one of the second schema must now be read in all three senses fitting for each of the definitions (other-same, species-genus, part-whole). In the final schema the many-one dichotomy is subordinated to the dichotomy between routine opinion and warranted opinion.

To follow the content as it appears linearly in the dialogue, the reader begins in the lower left corner, moves up the left-hand column, thence to the bottom of the middle column, then up that column, finally passing from the bottom of the right-hand column to the top. The arrows indicate the directions of movement. The carrying-over of basic dichotomies in the expanding context of the dialogue as one moves from the first through the second to the third schema helps convey a sense of unity of the argument as well as of the movement through the whole.

The unity in each schema is illustrated by the convergence of columns toward a common point—the point being beyond the structured multeity of the arguments themselves.

Though we make no claim that the formal structure as we have outlined it here really fixes once and for all the whole of Plato's argument (who could make such a claim?), we find it helpful for understanding the *Meno* and suggestive of the unity of Plato's dialectic as a whole. (For this latter point, see the final section of chap. 2).

We are indebted to Richard McKeon for having suggested the use of the lambda diagrams for indicating the divergence-convergence relations.

(ii)   *Schemata of Forms of Discourse*

The basic epistemological structuring of the dialogue is diagrammed in section i of this Appendix. Here we present schemata of the forms of discourse. They are variable; the elements designated in each form are not the only ones which could be emphasized, but at any rate they are all in the dialogue.

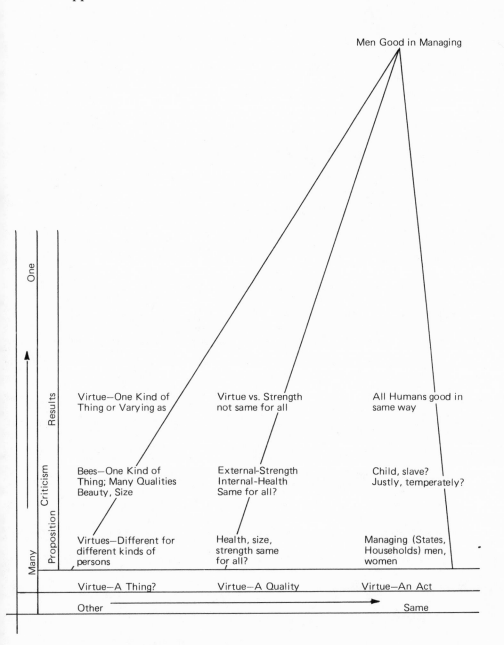

Men Good in Managing

One

Results

Criticism

Proposition

Many

Virtue—One Kind of
Thing or Varying as

Bees—One Kind of
Thing; Many Qualities
Beauty, Size

Virtues—Different for
different kinds of
persons

Virtue vs. Strength
not same for all

External-Strength
Internal-Health
Same for all?

Health, size,
strength same
for all?

All Humans good in
same way

Child, slave?
Justly, temperately?

Managing (States,
Households) men,
women

Virtue—A Thing?   Virtue—A Quality   Virtue—An Act

Other   Same

SCHEMA OF FIRST DEFINITION
(71E-72)

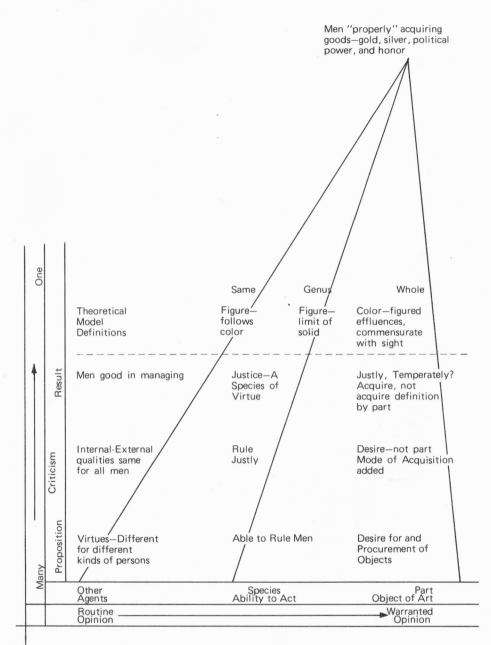

Men "properly" acquiring
goods—gold, silver, political
power, and honor

		Same	Genus	Whole
One				
	Theoretical Model Definitions	Figure—follows color	Figure—limit of solid	Color—figured effluences, commensurate with sight
Result	Men good in managing	Justice—A Species of Virtue		Justly, Temperately? Acquire, not acquire definition by part
Criticism	Internal-External qualities same for all men	Rule Justly		Desire—not part Mode of Acquisition added
Proposition	Virtues—Different for different kinds of persons	Able to Rule Men		Desire for and Procurement of Objects
Many	Other Agents	Species Ability to Act		Part Object of Art
	Routine Opinion			Warranted Opinion

SCHEMA OF DEFINITIONS
(71E–79E)

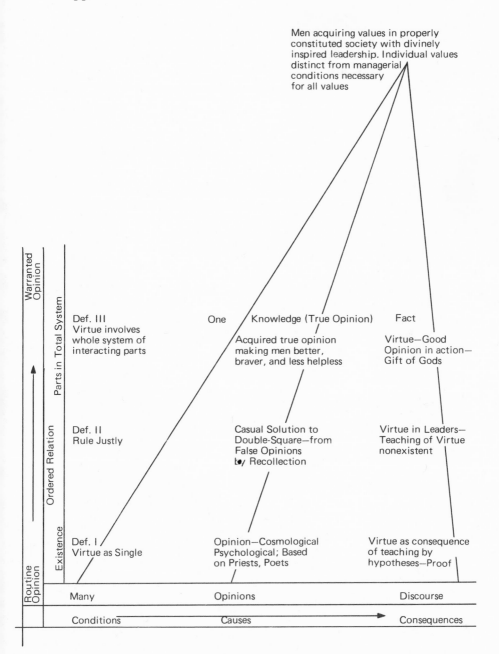

Men acquiring values in properly
constituted society with divinely
inspired leadership. Individual values
distinct from managerial
conditions necessary
for all values

Def. III Virtue involves whole system of interacting parts	One	Knowledge (True Opinion)	Fact
		Acquired true opinion making men better, braver, and less helpless	Virtue—Good Opinion in action— Gift of Gods
Def. II Rule Justly		Casual Solution to Double-Square—from False Opinions to Recollection	Virtue in Leaders— Teaching of Virtue nonexistent
Def. I Virtue as Single		Opinion—Cosmological Psychological; Based on Priests, Poets	Virtue as consequence of teaching by hypotheses—Proof
Many		Opinions	Discourse
Conditions		Causes	Consequences

Warranted Opinion

Parts in Total System

Ordered Relation

Existence

Routine Opinion

SCHEMA OF DIALOGUE

The main forms are compared below to show the culminating character of part III of the *Meno*, namely the relatively neglected inquiry into the acquisition of virtue. Compared with it, parts I and II are each one-sided. Part III combines their forms, though in attenuated versions, as argued in chapter 8, section i.

A. General Forms

Part of Dialogue	Leading Discussant's role	Sequential Segments	Outcome
I. EIDETIC (On definitions 71B–80B)	Authoritative Telling	Independently successful or unsuccessful universal propositions	Transmission of existent knowledge
II. HEURISTIC (Slave-boy episode— 80C–86B	Ostensive Questioning	Progressive stages of conceptual problem solving	Discovery of the unknown
III. DOXIC (On acquisition —86C–100B)	Guidance by telling/ questioning	Reformation of corrigible opinions	Persuasion to action

B. Specific Forms

I. EIDETIC

Form	Discussants	Starting Point	Process/Outcome
Eristic	Hostile	Opposed Meanings	Maintenance of an isolable universal
Dialectic	Friendly	Common Meanings	Agreement on a conceptually productive definition
Poetic	Appreciative	Invention	Pleasure in an explanatory system

II. HEURISTIC

The schema does not show the relation of the discussants involving Socrates' role as questioner, this being variously interpretable—a necessary feature of projections into the unknown.

Form	Starting Point	Process/Outcome
Pistic	Myth	Motivation to inquire
Zetetic	Aporia	Discovery of Cause
Reflective	Antecedent Achievement	Reinforced commitment to further inquiry

III. DOXIC GUIDANCE

Form	Discussants	Starting Point	Process/Outcome
Hypothetical	Teacher-Student	Hypothesis	Construction of deductive conclusion
Syzetetic	Persons pooling public facts	Empirical Survey	Public agreement on generalization
Persuasive Reasoning	Guide-guided	Incompatibility of theoretical and empirical findings	Persuasive resolution oriented to action

Notes

Preface

1. S. T. Coleridge, *Biographia Literaria* in *Selected Poetry and Prose of Coleridge*, ed. D. A. Stauffer (New York: Random House, 1951), p. 232.
2. Gilbert Ryle, "If Plato Only Knew," *New York Review of Books* 14, No. 8, 6 November 1965, p. 8.
3. Gilbert Ryle, *Plato's Progress* (Cambridge: Cambridge Univ. Press 1966), pp. 205 ff.
4. A. E. Taylor, *Plato the Man and His Work*, 5th ed. (London: Methuen, 1948), p. 130.
5. George Kimball Plochmann, *Plato* (New York: Dell, 1973), p. 30.

Introduction

1. The tradition begins at least as far back as Aristotle, cf. *Metaphysics* 1.6; 7.2. And both illuminating and controversial explanations or elaborations retain the emphasis. See, e.g., "The Development of Plato's Thought" in I. M. Crombie, *An Examination of Plato's Doctrines* (London: Routledge & Kegan Paul, 1962), I, 31–72, et passim; and chapters 3–9 of "The Spell of Plato" in Karl R. Popper. *The Open Society and Its Enemies* (Princeton, N.J.: Princeton Univ. Press, 1960), pp. 21–154.

2. R. G. Hoerber, "Plato's *Meno*," *Phronesis*, 5 (1960), 91.
3. Ibid., p. 100.
4. Jacob Klein, *A Commentary on Plato's Meno* (Chapel Hill, N.C.: Univ. of North Carolina Press, 1965), p. 250.
5. Victor Goldschmidt, *Les Dialogues de Platon: Structure et Method Dialectique*, 3rd ed. (Paris: Presses Universitaires de France, 1971), p. 128.
6. F. Schleiermacher, *Introduction to the Dialogues of Plato*, trans. W. Dobson (London: John Williams Parker, 1836), p. 211.
7. Klein, *Commentary*, p. 255.
8. H.-P. Stahl, "Beginnings of Propositional Logic in Plato," trans. Mrs. Gertrud Weiler from *Hermes* for *Plato's Meno*, ed. Malcolm Brown (Indianapolis: Bobbs-Merrill, 1971), p. 197.
9. Gilbert Ryle, *Plato's Progress* (Cambridge: Cambridge Univ. Press, 1966), pp. 205–11.
10. Bernard Phillips, "The Significance of *Meno*'s Paradox," in *Plato's Meno*, ed. Alexander Sesonske and Noel Fleming (Belmont, Calif.: Wadsworth, 1965), pp. 77–83.
11. Gregory Vlastos, "The Theory of Recollection in Plato's *Meno*," *Dialogue*, 4, No. 2 (Sept. 1965), 143–67 (Bobbs-Merrill, Reprint 215).
12. Malcolm Brown, "Plato Disapproves of the Slave-Boy's Answer," *Review of Metaphysics*, 21, No. 1 (Sept. 1967), 57–58. Jerome Eckstein also carries a similar negative view to an extreme, calling the episode a "farce." *The Platonic Method* (New York: Greenwood, 1968), p. 11.
13. Richard M. Hare, "Philosophical Discoveries," *Mind*, 69 (1960), 145–82. Also *Plato's Meno*, ed. Sesonske and Fleming, pp. 97–114.
14. Alexander Sesonske, "Knowing and Saying: The Structure of Plato's *Meno*," *Archiv für Philosophie*, 12 (1965). Also *Plato's Meno*, ed. Sesonske and Fleming, pp. 84–96.
15. Richard Robinson, *Plato's Earlier Dialectic*, 2nd ed. (Oxford: Clarendon Press, 1953), chap. 5.
16. Laura Grimm, *Definition in Plato's Meno* (Oslo: Oslo Univ. Press, 1962), p. 6.
17. Ernan McMullin, "Insight and the *Meno*," *Continuum*, 2, No. 3 (Autumn 1964), 369–73.
18. Ira Cohen, "Programmed Learning and the Socratic Dialogue," *American Psychologist*, 17 (1962), 772–75.
19. In English today this term has acquired a technical scientific meaning derived from its ordinary use in Greek. Our philosophic use of it retains the original sense of the cluster of meanings centering in "to come by," "to accrue to."
20. Klein, *Commentary*, p. 185. Though we criticize Klein's interpretation of the *Meno*, we have found his analyses generally illuminating.
21. Ibid., p. 35.
22. Gilbert Ryle, *Plato's Progress*, pp. 205, 220.
23. Robert S. Brumbaugh, "Plato's *Meno* as Form and as Content of Secondary School Courses in Philosophy," *Teaching Philosophy*, 1; No. 2 (Fall 1975), 107–15.
24. E. S. Thompson, ed. *The Meno of Plato* (London: Macmillan, 1901), p. xix.
25. John H. Randall, Jr., *Plato: Dramatist of the Life of Reason* (New York: Columbia Univ. Press, 1970), pp. 104.115.
26. For Randall, the whole dialogue is a dramatic commentary on the ideas of Gorgias through Meno as his product. The interpretation is argued

skillfully in line with Randall's view that Socrates himself mirrors the ideas of characters worth revealing. *Plato: Dramatist of the Life of Reason*, pp. 100, 104, 110–15. For us, Socrates does reflect but also critically extends Gorgias' method to engage Meno in a way of which Gorgias is incapable.

27. A sign is also given here of the limitation of the dialogue. When Meno expresses his preference for the inferior model, Socrates says Meno's judgment would be better if he remained for the mysteries (76E). An emotional seizure (*muethis*) is what Meno needs. The dialogue does about as much with him as a discourse can.

28. Klein, *Commentary*, p. 89.

29. Ibid., p. 255.

2. Definition and Dialectic in the *Meno*

1. Richard Robinson, *Plato's Earlier Dialectic*, 2nd ed. (Oxford: Clarendon Press, 1953), chap. 5, pp. 49–60. We find George Kimball Plochmann's more general and "looser" account of Plato's notion of dialectic much more pertinent to what is in the dialogues. *Plato* (New York: Dell 1973), pp. 102–16. Cf. also Gilbert Ryle, *Plato's Progress* (Cambridge: Cambridge Univ. Press, 1966).

2. A. E. Taylor, *Plato The Man and His Work*, 5th ed. (London: Methuen, 1948), p. 130.

3. Ibid., p. 130.

4. R. G. Hoerber, "Plato's *Meno*," *Phronesis*, 5 (1960), 83.

5. Virtue is learned by children as they learn their native tongue—taught by everyone who uses the language in their presence—327D–E.

6. I. M. Crombie says that this is an "unfortunate, not to say sophistical, analogy," since for Socrates " 'knowing what a thing is' is . . . the critical understanding of a general term." *An Examination of Plato's Doctrines* (London: Routledge & Kegan Paul, 1963), II, 532. Rather the analogy is one of the clues to the kind of knowledge being sought. Like Crombie, Jacob Klein makes assumptions which prevent one from seriously following up the clue: "If not to know (*gignōskein*) who Meno is, means never to have been introduced to him or never to have heard of him, the 'example' is not a valid one." *A Commentary on Plato's Meno* (Chapel Hill, N.C.: Univ. of North Carolina Press, 1965), p. 42.

7. Cf. Laura Grimm, *Definition in Plato's Meno* (Oslo: Oslo Univ. Press, 1962). She applies current logical and semantic categories, asks whether the definition Socrates seeks is nominal (descriptive or normative) or real (pp. 5–6) and finds Socrates confuses nominal and real definitions (pp. 30, 46). The general modern criticism that Plato neglects such distinctions, including use-mention, in defining terms overlooks the point that for Plato one does not define words, which are merely physical marks or sounds, but the concepts of the words as used in specified context. Cf. also George Kimball Plochmann, "Plato's *Meno*: Questions to be Disputed," *Journal of Value Inquiry*, 8, No. 4 (Winter 1974), 266–82. Plochmann's questions are more directly relevant to Plato's enterprise than are Grimm's categories.

8. E.g., Robinson, *Plato's Earlier Dialectic*, chap. 5.

9. We are generally indebted to Richard McKeon for teaching us that a man's method is integrally determinative of the significances to be given to his formulation and solution of problems, and for the comprehensive insight

that Platonic dialectic is best understood as a definitional dialectic with methodological unity. We are particularly indebted to him for suggestions for improving our interpretation of the *Meno* at several points—for example, it was his suggestion that we contrast the *ti-poion* dialogues with the *ti-poson, ti-pōs,* and *ti (Republic)* dialogues.

3. The Slave-Boy Episode

1. W. H. D. Rouse, trans. *Great Dialogues of Plato,* ed. Eric M. Warminton and Phillip G. Rouse (New York: Mentor, 1956), p. 41. Cf. Plato's *Euthydemus* 278D–279C.
2. *Posterior Analytics* 2.71a27. Aristotle notes the difference in the *Meno* from knowing a universal and knowing the applicability of the universal to all the particular cases to which it applies. His solution of the problem of knowing the universal consists of the intuition of first truths of a science—these stating the nature of the object of inquiry, this being also the cause of the properties of the object (chap. 19). The *Meno* presents a different, though related, solution in which discovery as acquaintance knowledge, distinct from descriptive opinion, does involve the causal connection.
3. Some of the recent commentary: R. E. Allen, "Anamnesis in Plato's *Meno* and *Phaedo*," *Review of Metaphysics,* 13, No. 1 (Sept. 1959), 165–74. Malcolm Brown, "Plato Disapproves of the Slave-Boy's Answer," *Review of Metaphysics,* 21, No. 1 (Sept. 1967), 57–93. Robert S. Brumbaugh, *Plato's Mathematical Imagination* (Bloomington, Ind.: Indiana Univ. Press, 1954), pp. 21–32. Richard M. Hare, "Plato and the Mathematicians," in *New Essays on Plato and Aristotle,* ed. R. Bambrough (London: Routledge & Kegan Paul, 1965). Hare also has an article, "Philosophic Discoveries," in *Plato's Meno,* ed. Alexander Sesonske and Noel Fleming (Belmont, Calif.: Wadsworth, 1965), pp. 97–114. Julius Moravcsik, "Learning as Recollection," in *Plato: I,* ed. Gregory Vlastos (Garden City, N.Y.: Doubleday Anchor Books, 1971). Bernard Phillips, "The Significance of Meno's Paradox," in *Plato's Meno,* ed. Sesonske and Fleming, pp. 77–83. Sir David Ross, *Plato's Theory of Ideas* (Oxford: Clarendon Press, 1961). A. E. Taylor, *Plato the Man and His Work* (New York: Dial Press, 1936). Gregory Vlastos, "The Theory of Recollection in Plato's *Meno*," *Dialogue,* 4, No. 2 (1965), 143–67, also in Bobbs-Merrill Reprint 215. Nicholas P. White, "Inquiry," *Review of Metaphysics,* 28, No. 2 (Dec. 1974), 289–310.
4. Brown, "Plato Disapproves of the Slave-Boy's Answer."
5. Vlastos, "The Theory of Recollection in Plato's *Meno*." Vlastos suggests that Cornford, Guthrie, Bluck, Gulley, and Crombie side with his rationalist interpretation whereas Ross and Taylor are mistaken in their empiricist learnings.
6. Vlastos, "The Theory of Recollection."
7. Brown, "Plato Disapproves."
8. This is assumed by such diverse interpretations as those of Brown, Hare, and Vlastos.
9. Various commentators have treated this passage as consisting of two or three parts. For example, Malcolm Brown distinguishes two experiments. Further, he has argued the radical difference of the two experiments on questionable grounds to prove a "fact" about the state of geometry which

Plato was presumably exposing. The "fact" is dubious at best and inadequate for understanding the history of mathematics and a viable philosophy of mathematics. See note 20 below.

10. Cf. Moravcsik, "Learning as Recollection," p. 57.
11. A. N. Whitehead, *Science and the Modern World* (New York: Macmillan, 1947), p. 38.
12. Cf. Vlastos, "The Theory of Recollection."
13. George Kimball Plochmann has noted that the slave-boy has some power of abstraction; for even in the first experiment he accepts units of measure in general rather than the actual inches on the ground.
14. A. E. Taylor, *Plato*, p. 138, n. 2.
15. Brown, "Plato Disapproves," pp. 66–67.
16. Vlastos, "The Theory of Recollection," p. 154.
17. Ibid., p. 154*n*. There is sufficient philosophic tradition for the use of "cause" in a non-Humean sense, so no defense of this translation of "aitia" is needed. Cf. Hobbes, Leibniz, Kant, etc. Cf. R. J. Collingwood, *Essay on Metaphysics* (Chicago: Henry Regnery, 1972), pt. 3C.
18. Karl R. Popper, "The Nature of Philosophical Problems and Their Roots in Science," in *Plato's Meno*, ed. Malcolm Brown (Indianapolis, Ind.: Bobbs-Merrill, 1971), p. 161.
19. Jacob Klein, *A Commentary on Plato's Meno* (Chapel Hill, N.C.: Univ. of North Carolina Press, 1965) pp. 177–79. There is linguistic support of this where Socrates, referring to the slave-boy's prenatal possession of the geometric opinions, says that "it is obvious that he had them and learnt them during some other time" (86A1–2—Lamb). The point, puzzling apart from the position we have set forth, is that having them and having learnt them are treated as compatible with his having always had them.
20. Cf. George Kimball Plochmann, "Plato's *Meno*: Questions to be Disputed," *Journal of Value Inquiry*, 8, No. 4 (Winter 1974), 279. Eudoxus' definition of "magnitudes being in the same ratio" as it comes to us in Euclid's *Elements* (Bk. 5, Def. 5) constitutes the basis for the general ancient solution to the ordering of incommensurables. However, the historian of mathematics, Eudemus (ca. 355 B.C.), credited Hippocrates of Chios, praised as the most rigorous mathematician of the fifth century B.C., with proving that similar segments of circles are *in the same ratio* as the squares of their bases (B. L. Van der Waerden, *Science Awakening*, trans. A. Dresden [New York: Oxford Univ. Press, 1961], p. 132—also *Elements*, Bk. 12, Prop. 2), though our only evidence for how he achieved this is derived from his work on squaring a lunule.

Van der Waerden attributes an earlier definition of proportion (in terms of "taking away"—*antanairesis*) to Theaetetus, though he uses the notion of "taking away" in his reconstruction of why Theodorus (Theaetetus' teacher) stopped his inquiry into incommensurable lengths with the square root of 17. Eudoxus' achievement evidently overshadowed the earlier definition which is not referred to in the *Elements*. But it is also not referred to in Plato's *Theaetetus* where Socrates praises Theaetetus for his general definitions and classifications of different kinds of lengths (also *Elements*, Bk. 10), Aristotle's reference to this definition (*Topics* 158B) clearly allows the possibility that it originated earlier than Theaetetus or Theodorus, and may go back to Hippocrates or beyond.

Though it is unknown how rigorous Hippocrates' proofs were, whether he stated an axiom on proportions for continuous quantities, or if he defined "proportion" in terms of "taking away," clearly his use of the same ratio shows that his ideas were applicable to magnitudes. Further, the best evidence supports the belief that the incommensurability of the side and diagonal of a square had been proved early in fifth century B.C. Therefore it is not clear why Van der Waerden attributes the "taking away" definition to Theaetetus and holds that Hippocrates' notion of a part had to apply to rational ratios and commensurable magnitudes only.

But more to the point of our immediate concern with the *Meno*, Malcolm Brown, "Plato Disapproves," imports the problem of incommensurables into the dialogue, uses the shadowy history of the early theory of proportions and the shadowy history of Plato's writing his dialogues to fix a date for the *Meno* (not later than 386 B.C.) and to interpret the slave-boy episode as somehow constituting a criticism of the state of mathematics at that time, though the evidence is that mathematics was not in such a state at that time and though Plato's language is forced to bear unwarranted significances and Plato's argument is distorted in order to have the slave-boy episode perform this presumed critical function.

21. Van der Waerden, *Science Awakening*, p. 125.
22. Ibid., p. 126.
23. Arpad Szabo, "The Transformation of Mathematics into Deductive Science and the Beginnings of its Foundations on Definitions and Axioms," *Scripta Mathematica*, 27, Nos. 1 and 2 (1964), pp. 27–48A and 113–38.
24. Neugebauer, Tannery, Zeuthen, Heath, Sacks, Becker, Toeplitz, Reidmeister, and others built a solid picture of early Greek mathematics despite the fact that much was lost because Euclid's *Elements* superseded the earlier work. This is attested to by Van der Waerden, *Science Awakening*, and Asger Aaboe, *Episodes from the Early History of Mathematics* (New York: Random House and L. W. Singer, 1964), pp. 37–38.
25. Also see Robert S. Brumbaugh, *Plato's Mathematical Imagination* (Bloomington, Ind.: Indiana Univ. Press, 1954).
26. Cf. R. E. Allen, "Anamnesis in Plato's *Meno* and *Phaedo*." Also see R. Hackforth, *Plato's Phaedo* (New York: Liberal Arts Press, n.d.), p. 76. Cf. also Plochmann, "Plato's *Meno*," p. 273. He doubts the validity of a literal cross-reference.
27. We are indebted to Nathaniel Lawrence for pressing and exploring this issue with us.

4. Can Virtue Be Acquired by Being Taught?

1. Jerome Eckstein, *The Platonic Method* (New York: Greenwood, 1968), pp. 37 ff.
2. Cf. George Kimball Plochmann, "Plato's *Meno*: "Questions to be Disputed," *Journal of Value Inquiry*, 8, No. 4 (Winter 1974), p. 278.
3. "Plato's *Meno* 89C: 'Virtue is Knowledge'—A Hypothesis?" *Phronesis* 21.2 (1976), pp. 130–34, and "Plato's *Meno* 86E–87A: The Geometrical Illustration of the Argument by Hypothesis," *Phronesis*, in press. Also cf. Robert S. Brumbaugh, *Plato's Mathematical Imagination* (Bloomington, Ind.: Indiana Univ. Press, 1954), pp. 32–38.
4. W. H. D. Rouse, trans., *Great Dialogues of Plato*, ed. Eric H. Warminton and Phillip G. Rouse (New York: Mentor Books, 1965), p. 52. Our primary commentary source has been R. S. Bluck, *Plato's Meno* (Cambridge:

Cambridge Univ. Press, 1964), pp. 441–61. Additional commentaries by S. H. Butcher, Thomas L. Heath, Ivor Thomas, and E. S. Thompson have been used.

5. W. R. M. Lamb, trans., Loeb Classical Library (Cambridge, Mass: Harvard Univ. Press, 1962), p. 333. This reading of this passage apparently has universal acceptance, being expressed and developed with slight variations by such commentators as Harold Cherniss, Paul Friedländer, Richard Robinson, R. S. Bluck, Lynn E. Rose, and H.-P. Stahl. Cf. also Sir David Ross, *Plato's Theory of Ideas* (Oxford: Clarendon Press, 1951), p. 29, who presents this argument as "in fact the appropriate method of discovering the proof of mathematical theorems," whereas Plato presents this as the application of mathematical theorems to a case at hand.

6. The joint assertion of "If Virtue is knowledge, virtue is teachable" and "Virtue is knowledge" logically entails "Virtue is teachable."

7. Richard S. Rudner, *Philosophy of Social Sciences* (Englewood Cliffs, N.J.: Prentice-Hall, 1966), p. 3. We are not denying that for Russell as for Plato (slave-boy episode and *Republic* V–VII) pursuit of knowledge is an ultimate good for man. Bertrand Russell, *The Problems of Philosophy* (London: Oxford Univ. Press, 1959), pp. 158–61 and "A Free Man's Worship," in *Selected Papers of Bertrand Russell* (New York: Random House, 1927), pp. 1–15.

5. The Anytos Episode A: Structure of the Argument

1. We follow Klein in using this label to cover the whole exchange from 90B to 96D, which includes the discussion with Meno on whether virtue is taught in Thessaly. Jacob Klein, *A Commentary on Plato's Meno* (Chapel Hill, N.C.: Univ. of North Carolina Press, 1965), p. 226.

2. R. G. Hoerber, "Plato's *Meno*," *Phronesis* 5 (1960), 90.

3. R. S. Bluck, *Plato's Meno* (Cambridge: Cambridge Univ. Press, 1964), pp. 29–30.

4. Klein, *Commentary*, p. 236.

5. Victor Goldschmidt, *Les Dialogues de Platon: Structure et Method Dialectique*, 3rd ed. (Paris: Presses Universitaires de France, 1971), p. 128.

6. F. M. Cornford, *Plato and Parmenides* (London: Routledge & Kegan Paul, 1939), p. 245.

7. A. E. Taylor, *Plato the Man and His Work*, 5th ed. (London: Methuen, 1948), pp. 140–43.

8. B. F. Skinner, *Walden Two* (New York: Macmillan, 1948). After enumerating goods as objects of knowledge (pp. 159 ff.), Frazier, the protagonist in the book, says their totality as the good life is "a fact" (p. 161), and is achievable by "behavioral engineering" (p. 162) as part of a "science of behavior" (p. 175).

9. Bluck, *Plato's Meno*, p. 128.

10. Hoerber's criticism that the "claim that sophists and the Athenian statesmen exhaust the possibilities of discovering teachers of virtue is very unsound" misses just this operational condition or assurance which the Anytos episode requires. Hoerber, "Plato's *Meno*," p. 91.

11. Klein, *Commentary*, p. 240.

12. Goldschmidt, *Le Dialogues de Platon*, pp. 125 ff.

13. Since at the dictionary level *didakton* "expresses what *has been* done" (Rev. Francis M. Connell, S.J., *A Short Grammar of Attic Greek* [Boston: Allyn and Bacon, 1919] par. no. 402, p. 169), and since translators accordingly vary their renderings from taught to teachable, we depend on our analysis of the term, rather than on the one-word translation we use, to convey our interpretation.

14. This sequence of three quotations is taken from the Lamb translation.

15. *Phrasas*, better rendered as "showing the way." *Greek-English Lexicon*, 9th ed., comp. Henry George Liddell and Robert Scott (Oxford: Clarendon Press, 1940), p. 1952.

16. Socrates says ironically that Anytos "knows" (*eidenai*—91B) the sophists to be teachers (since they satisfy the criteria of professing and being successful). But in doing so Socrates is enabled to make a special point whose principle later comes to be important. When Anytos repudiates the sophists, Socrates establishes that he is "without experience" of them, and *for that reason* cannot know them (92C). Thus in this relevant use of "know" it is tied to experience; and in the final section of the dialogue as we show in chapter 7, experience turns out to be the basis of the knowledge which the virtuous man lacks.

17. Klein, *Commentary*, p. 226.

18. Bluck, *Plato's Meno*, p. 367.

19. The emphasis on the lack of power in the precept is evident from the contrast Theognis draws between making a man good and teaching him. Theognis' attention is on power in a different but still related sense when he says also what Socrates takes as favoring teachability: "be pleasing to them who wield great power; for from the good wilt thou win thee lessons in the good" (95D–E).

20. Immanuel Kant, *Critique of Judgement*, trans. Bernard (New York: Hafner, 1951), p. 150.

21. *Sophron* characterizes public judgment in these arts, as noted earlier. The connotation it carries of a sanity which is moderate, avoiding extremes, puts the stress on continuity of results in the products rather than single exceptional or flukish cases.

22. Compare Aristotle's reference to Theognis in the context of his treatment of legislation to inculcate human excellence. *Nicomachean Ethics* 10.9. 1179b5.

23. A. E. Taylor, *Plato the Man and His Work*, p. 141.

24. A note on Thucydides. In crediting him with virtue in the use of resources rather than with the sort of giant contributions of the other three, we may seem to slight him (see e.g., Aristotle *Athenisium Respublica* 28, 5 [Oxford: Clarendon Press, 1921]). But this fits the treatment of him in the *Meno*. In contrast to the other three, his virtue is not affirmed explicitly, though it is indicated; and his function in the argument is different from theirs. They are presented as serial items in an induction, each having had sons who were not taught virtue. Then the three are looked at together retrospectively (94B), and Thucydides is introduced to complete the induction, not simply as the last in the series but as the man who had the friends, lineage, and affluence to have found a teacher for his sons if one existed anywhere in Greece. We see his political conservatism as likewise notable in the judgment concerning the use of the state's resources. This interpretation does not affect the basic point we are making here about the virtue of Athens' leaders.

6. The Anytos Episode B: The Economics of Virtue

1. Karl R. Popper, *The Open Society and Its Enemies* (Princeton: Princeton Univ. Press, 1950), p. 126.
2. Aristotle *Rhetoric* 1. 1356a.
3. Cf. A. N. Whitehead, *Adventures of Ideas* (New York: Free Press, 1967), pt. 1 and pp. 130, 169–71, 208.
4. A. E. Taylor, *Plato the Man and His Work*, 5th ed. (London: Methuen, 1948), p. 141.
5. Evidence for this rests partly on the final exchange in the dialogue (99D–E), where there is a difference of opinion as to which persons speak which lines. We take W. R. M. Lamb's judgment on this. Loeb Classical Library (Cambridge, Mass.: Harvard Univ. Press, 1962), p. 263. Our chief basis for the response we attribute hypothetically to Anytos is the total role he plays and attitudes he shows.

7. Knowing and Opining Particular Facts

1. I. M. Crombie, *An Examination of Plato's Doctrines*, II, 53 (London: Routledge & Kegan Paul, 1963), speaks of the importance of acquaintance here, though not as it is intended to mark out specific features of knowledge of particulars as distinct from knowledge of mathematical theorems. R. S. Bluck perceptively notes that the point of the "much maligned" illustration of the road to Larisa is "simply that knowledge involves personal acquaintance whereas true belief does not." "Plato's *Meno*," *Phronesis*, 6 (1961), 100. See also *Plato's Meno*, ed. R. S. Bluck (Cambridge: Cambridge Univ. Press, 1964), p. 32. Bluck also emphasizes the parallelism between the double square problem and the road to Larisa, but unfortunately he slights the distinctive features of each kind of cognition.

8. Forms of Discourse, Approximative Method and Operational Structure

1. Aristotle *Metaphysics* 1. 987B: *Posterior Analytics* 2. 71A.
2. Aristotle denies that Empedocles was a poet and says that his verses do not make him one (*Poetics* 447B). Plato associates him with poets because of the inventive character of his physics (76C–E).
3. The labels used throughout for the forms of discourse are generally drawn from the Greek terms Plato chooses, and the references given are to the original. See Appendix, sec. ii for summary of forms of discourse.
4. E.g., Gilbert Ryle, "Systematically Misleading Expressions," in *Logic and Language*, First Series, ed. Anthony Flew (Garden City, N.Y.: Doubleday, 1965), pp. 13–40.
5. Robert K. Merton, *The Sociology of Science* (Chicago: Univ. of Chicago Press, 1973), pp. 352 ff.

9. General Paragenics

1. Russell shifts from an appearance-reality distinction into an acquaintance-description distinction. See chaps. 1–5, *The Problems of*

Philosophy (London: Oxford Univ. Press, 1959), originally published in 1912.

2. Cf. William James on acquaintance knowledge and knowledge about, in *Essays in Radical Empiricism and A Pluralistic Universe* (New York: Longmans, Green, 1947), pp. 54, 68, 73. Note his interpretation of Bergson in the acquaintance-description framework, pp. 225–73. Gustav Bergmann insists on taking account of awarenesses (acquaintances) in an ideal language with appropriate descriptive devices—such an interpreted syntactical schema providing the cognitive philosophical structure adequate to the totality of man's experience; see *The Metaphysics of Logical Positivism* (New York: Longmans, Green, 1954), chaps. 1–6. Also, *Meaning and Existence* (Madison: Univ. of Wisconsin Press, 1960), chap. 1.

3. Cf. Paul Hayner, "Knowledge by Acquaintance," *Philosophy and Phenomenological Research*, 29 (March 1969), 423–31, esp. p. 423.

4. G. Dawes Hicks criticized this notion because all knowledge is discursive and Russell's acquaintance knowledge is not, "Symposium: Is There Knowledge by Acquaintance?" *Aristotelean Society Proceedings*, Supplementary Vol. II, 159–78. G. E. Moore and C. D. Broad accepted the notion as mere common sense, ibid., pp. 179–93 and 206–20 respectively. H. L. A. Hart accepted it as mere common sense like "knowing by heart," "Symposium: Is There Knowledge by Acquaintance?" *Aristotelean Society Proceedings*, Supplementary Vol. XXI, 69–90. J. N. Findlay defended acquaintance knowledge as a technical extension beyond common sense, thus opening up new technical insights into objects known, ibid., pp. 111–28.

5. Reinhardt Grossman, *Ontological Reduction* (Bloomington, Ind.: Indiana Univ. Press, 1973), p. 4. Cf. his treatment of acquaintance knowledge of individuals in contrast to Berkeley's and Goodman's constructionisms.

6. Hayner, "Knowledge by Acquaintence," pp. 429–31.

7. G. E. Hughes, "Symposium," *Aristotelean Society Proceedings*, Vol. XXI, esp. pp. 100 ff. J. N. Findlay expresses "particular admiration" for Hughes' insight, ibid., Vol. XXI, p. 116.

8. F. H. Bradley, *The Principles of Logic* (London: Oxford Univ. Press, 1922), chap. 1.

9. F. H. Bradley, *Essays on Truth and Reality* (Oxford: Clarendon Press, 1944), chap. 6.

10. P. F. Strawson, *Individuals* (Garden City, N.Y.: Doubleday, 1963).

11. Cf. F. H. Bradley, *Essays on Truth and Reality*, pp. 166 ff. and John Dewey, *Experience and Nature*, 2nd ed. (1929; rpt. La Salle, Ill.: Open Court, 1961), chap. 6.

12. A. N. Whitehead, *Process and Reality* (1929; rpt. New York: Social Science Book Store, 1941), p. 124.

13. Cf. Saul Kripke, "Naming and Necessity," *Semantics of Natural Languages*, ed. G. Harman and D. Davidson (Vordrecht: Reide, 1972). Kripke argues the necessity in the identity sentence using proper names, and extends this to such theoretical identities, using the example given here repeatedly, pp. 303, 304, 323, 325, 326, 330.

14. Cf. Immanuel Kant, *Critique of Pure Reason*, trans. F. M. Müller (New York: Macmillan, 1934), especially the "Transcendental Aesthetic" and "Transcendental Analytic." Noam Chomsky, *Language and Mind* (New York: Harcourt, Brace & World, 1968).

15. H. Poincaré, *The Foundations of Science*, trans. G. B. Halstead (Lancaster,

Pa.: Science Press, 1946), pp. 383–94. Cf. Plato's *Theaetetus*, the analogy of ideas in the mind to birds in an aviary.

16. Ludwig Wittgenstein, *Philosophical Investigations*, trans. G. E. M. Anscombe (New York: Macmillan, 1968), pp. 1–51.

17. Gilbert Ryle, *The Concept of Mind* (New York: Barnes & Noble, 1949), p. 44.

18. N. R. Hanson, *Perception and Discovery*, ed. Willard C. Humphreys (San Francisco: Freeman, Cooper, 1969), pp. 61 ff., 245 ff. William James, *Essays in Radical Empiricism*, Essay 1.

19. Michael A. Slote, *Reason and Scepticism* (New York: Humanities Press, 1970).

20. John Dewey, *Experience and Nature*, p. 201. P. F. Strawson, *Individuals*, pp. 100–112. Ludwig Wittgenstein, *Tractatus Logico-Philosophicus* trans. D. F. Pears and B. F. McGuinness (London: Routledge & Kegan Paul, 1961), paragraph number 5.6 ff.

21. Erwin Schrödinger, *What Is Life?* (Cambridge: Cambridge Univ. Press, 1937). Cf. Lucretius, *On the Nature of Things*, trans. H. A. J. Munro (New York: Washington Square Press, 1956), p. 36.

22. Rudolf Carnap, *Philosophy and Logical Syntax* (London: Kegan Paul, Trench, Trubner, 1937). C. G. Hempel, *Philosophy of Natural Science* (Englewood Cliffs, N.J.: Prentice-Hall, 1966). Ernest Nagel, *The Structure of Science* (New York: Harcourt, Brace & World), 1961). R. B. Braithwaite, *Scientific Explanation* (Cambridge: Cambridge Univ. Press, 1955).

23. Logical inquiries into proof theory (formal syntax) and the semantics of science abound. Reduction of intentional elements to syntactically and semantically clarified elements is one basic aim, while pragmatic assumptions underlie the whole enterprise. A recurring interesting controversy is that involving the combination of the atemporal structure of the logic of science with the irreducible element in all scientific prediction. Cf. Adolf Grünbaum, *Philosophical Problems of Space and Time* (New York: Knopf, 1963), pp. 290 ff. Cf. Nelson Goodman, *Fact, Fiction and Forecast* (New York: Bobbs-Merrill, 1965). Also see Stephen Toulmin, *The Philosophy of Science* (New York: Harper & Row, 1953) and *Foresight and Understanding* (New York: Harper & Row, 1961), for an experiential historical treatment of scientific explanation. For him, prediction is low-level projection from empirical generalizations, requiring explanation based on ideals of natural order for proper understanding.

Various accounts of scientific explanation turn on diverse elements within the total structure of scientific description. For examples, scientific explanation is variously characterized as hypothetical-deductive (Braithwaite), deductive-nomological (Hempel), statistical-relevance (Reichenbach), or involving falsifiable propositions (Popper).

24. G. E. Moore, *Principia Ethica* (Cambridge: Cambridge Univ. Press, 1968), pp. 1–17.

25. Richard M. Hare, *The Language of Morals* (Oxford: Clarendon Press, 1952), also his *Freedom and Reason* (New York: Oxford Univ. Press, 1965).

26. Charles L. Stevenson, *Ethics and Language* (New Haven: Yale Univ. Press, 1944), chaps. 1, 2, 4, and *Facts and Values* (New Haven: Yale Univ. Press, 1963), chaps. 1–4.

27. J. L. Austin, "Ifs and Cans," in *The Nature of Human Action*, ed. Myles Brand (Glenview, Ill.: Scott, Foresman, 1970), pp. 161–78.

28. Ibid., p. 178.

29. Cf. P. H. Nowell-Smith, "Freedom and Responsibility," in *The Nature of*

Human Action, ed. Myles Brand, pp. 157–60. Also Storrs McCall, "Ability as a Species of Possibility," ibid., pp. 139–147.

30. Arthur C. Danto, "Basic Actions," and "What We Can Do," in *Readings in the Theory of Action* ed. N. S. Core and C. Landesman, (Bloomington: Indiana Univ. Press, 1968), pp. 93–126.

31. H. L. A. Hart and A. M. Honore, *Causation in the Law* (Oxford: Clarendon Press, 1959), p. 2.

32. Ibid., p. 52. Cf. also, R. G. Collingwood, *An Essay on Metaphysics* (Chicago: Henry Regnery, 1972), chaps. 29 and 30.

33. Ibid., pt. 2, chap. 9.

34. Cf. John R. Silber, "Human Action and the Language of Volitions," in *Readings in Theory of Action,* ed. Norman S. Core and Charles Landesman (Bloomington: Indiana Univ. Press, 1968), pp. 68–92. Note Silber's argument for unity of will and action in a completed action as contrasted with their separations in incomplete actions, pp. 83 ff. Both are described retrospectively. For a paragenic notion of foresight, see A. N. Whitehead, *Adventures of Ideas* (New York: Free Press, 1961), chap. 6. This contrasts sharply with Toulmin's use of this term as a mere extension of empirical regularities, *Foresight and Understanding,* chap. 2.

35. Donald Davidson, "Actions, Reasons and Causes," in *The Nature of Human Action,* pp. 67–79.

36. Stuart Hampshire, *Thought and Action* (New York: Viking Press, 1967).

37. Ibid., pp. 132 ff; 255 ff.

38. Ibid., p. 166.

39. Ibid., pp. 133, 256–69, 272–73.

40. Paul Ricoeur, "The Unity of the Voluntary and the Involuntary as a Limiting Idea," in *Readings in Existential Phenomenology,* ed. N. Lawrence and D. J. O'Connor (Englewood Cliffs, N.J.: Prentice-Hall, 1967), pp. 93–112—esp. pp. 93, 95.

41. Paul Ricoeur, "The Antinomy of Human Reality and the Problem of Philosophical Anthropology," in *Readings in Existential Phenomenology,* pp. 390–402.

42. Ibid., p. 402. For contrast cf. William James, "The Experience of Activity," in *Essays in Radical Empiricism and a Pluralistic Universe.*

43. Karl Jaspers, *Way to Wisdom* (New Haven: Yale Univ. Press, 1968), pp. 19–20.

44. Jean-Paul Sartre, *Existentialism* (New York: Philosophical Library, 1947), p. 20.

45. Robert Nozick, *Anarchy, State, and Utopia* (New York: Basic Books, 1974), chaps. 3 and 5.

46. Alexander Bickel, *The Morality of Consent* (New Haven: Yale Univ. Press, 1974–75), pp. 3–30. Also see Wasserstrom's citations from Bickel, note 47 below.

47. Richard Wasserstrom, "Contempt of Court," *New York Review of Books,* 15, No. 2, (7 Jan. 1971), p. 18.

48. B. F. Skinner, *Walden Two* (New York: Macmillan, 1948).

49. Theodore Roosevelt, *The Works of Theodore Roosevelt,* Mem. Edn. (New York: Charles Scribner's Sons, 1923–25), XV, 57.

50. John Rawls, *A Theory of Justice* (Cambridge, Mass.: Harvard Univ. Press, 1971), p. 31.

51. David Hume, *An Enquiry Concerning the Principles of Morals,* in *Essential Works of David Hume,* ed. R. Cohen (New York: Bantam Books, 1965), pp. 191–92; and Rawls, *A Theory of Justice,* p. 33.

52. Nicholas Rescher, *Distributive Justice* (Indianapolis, Ind.: Bobbs-Merrill, 1966), p. 120.
53. Rawls, *A Theory of Justice*, p. 12.
54. Ibid., pp. 8–9.
55. Robert Nozick, *Anarchy, State, and Utopia*, pp. 150–53.
56. Edmund Husserl, *Ideas*, trans. W. R. Boyce Gibson (New York: Collier Books, 1962), sec. nos. 9–16, 63–75, 146 ff.
57. William James, "Does Consciousness Exist?" *Essays in Radical Empiricism*, Essay 1.
58. F. H. Bradley, *Principles of Logic*, p. 10; A. N. Whitehead, *Process and Reality*, pt. 3.
59. John Dewey, *Experience and Nature*, p. 84.
60. Gustav Bergmann, "Logical Positivism, Language and the Reconstruction of Metaphysics," and "Bodies, Minds, and Acts," in *The Metaphysics of Logical Positivism*. Also "Intentionality," in *Meaning and Existence*.
61. Karl R. Popper, *The Logic of Scientific Discovery* (New York: Harper & Row, 1965). Also *The Open Society and Its Enemies* Princeton, N.J.: Princeton Univ. Press, 1950), p. 121. "I am inclined to think that rulers have rarely been above average, either morally or intellectually, and often below it."
62. Ludwig Wittgenstein, *Philosophical Investigations* (New York: Macmillan, 1953), paragraph number 122.
63. P. F. Strawson, *Individuals*, chaps. 1, 3. Cf. also William James in his many accounts of the selves, bodies, physical world as spatial-temporal, consciousness, etc., in *Essays in Radical Empiricism*.
64. William James, *Pragmatism* (New York: Longmans, Green, 1961), pp. 79–81; A. N. Whitehead, *Science and the Modern World* (New York: Macmillan, 1947), chap. 11.
65. Edmund Husserl, *Ideas*, sec. nos. 72–75.
66. Wilfrid Sellars, *Science, Perception, and Reality.* (London: Routledge & Kegan Paul, 1963), pp. 32–37.
67. John Dewey, *Logic, The Theory of Inquiry* (New York: Henry Holt, 1938), chaps. 1–6.
68. Maurice Merleau-Ponty, *The Primacy of Perception*, ed. James Edie (Evanston, Ill.: Northwestern Univ. Press, 1964), p. 16. He also treats thought as a similar combination of focal-background content. For example, note his treatment of Meno's paradox in *The Phenomenology of Perception*, trans. Colin Smith (London: Routledge & Kegan Paul, 1962), pp. 370–71.
69. A. N. Whitehead, *Science and the Modern World*, chap. 1. Whitehead argues the dominant role of Newtonian-Cartesian thought in the cosmological thought of the past three centuries.
70. Francis Bacon, *Advancement of Learning and Novum Organon*, ed. J. E. Creighton, rev. ed. (New York: Colonial Press, 1890), p. 315.
71. John Dewey, *Experience and Nature*, chap. 2, and Jean-Paul Sartre, *Being and Nothingness*, trans. Hazel E. Barnes, (New York: Philosophical Library, 1956), pt. 4.
72. Cf. note 64 above.
73. The impact of Darwinian evolutionary theory on late nineteenth- and early twentieth-century philosophy (Spencer, Bergson, Whitehead, etc.) is well known. The advent of a more recent discoveries in reproduction (DNA, etc.) sparked a resurgence of evolutionary philosophies (Monod, Jacob, etc.).

74. Stephen Toulmin, *Foresight and Understanding*. Cf. also T. S. Kuhn, *The Structure of Scientific Revolutions* (Chicago: Univ. of Chicago Press, 1967). Toulmin's looser treatment of the history of science seems to fit the contours of fact more easily, while Kuhn's treatment seems to echo the philosophical role science played during the modern period. Cf. Whitehead, note 69 above.

Index

171